SHAMBHALA DRAGON EDITIONS

The dragon is an age-old symbol of the highest spiritual essence, embodying wisdom, strength, and the divine power of transformation. In this spirit, Shambhala Dragon Editions offers a treasury of readings in the sacred knowledge of Asia. In presenting the works of authors both ancient and modern, we seek to make these teachings accessible to lovers of wisdom everywhere.

Books by Thomas Cleary

The Japanese Art of War: Understanding the Culture of Strategy (1991)*

I CHING STUDIES
The Taoist I Ching, by Liu I-ming (1986)*
The Buddhist I Ching, by Chih-hsu Ou-i (1987)*
I Ching: The Tao of Organization, by Cheng Yi (1988)*
I Ching Mandalas: A Program of Study for The Book of Changes (1989)*
I Ching: The Book of Change (1992)*

TAOIST STUDIES
The Inner Teachings of Taoism, by Chang Po-tuan (1986)*
The Art of War, by Sun Tzu (1988)*
Awakening to the Tao, by Liu I-ming (1988)*
The Book of Balance and Harmony (1989)
Immortal Sisters: Secrets of Taoist Women (1989)*
Mastering the Art of War, by Zhuge Liang & Liu Ji (1989)*
Back to Beginnings: Reflections on the Tao (1990)*
*The Tao of Politics: Lessons of the Masters of Huainan**
Further Teachings of Lao Tzu: Understanding the Mysteries (1991)*
*Vitality, Energy, Spirit: A Taoist Sourcebook**
The Essential Tao (1992)*

BUDDHIST STUDIES
The Blue Cliff Record (1977)*
The Flower Ornament Scripture, 3 vols. (1984–1987)*
Shobogenzo: Zen Essays by Dogen (1986)
The Book of Serenity (1989)
Entry into the Realm of Reality: The Text (1989)*
Entry into the Realm of Reality: The Guide, by Li Tongxuan (1989)*
Zen Essence: The Science of Freedom (1989)*
Zen Lessons: The Art of Leadership (1989)*
Transmission of Light, by Zen Master Keizan (1990)
The Book of Serenity: One Hundred Zen Dialogues (1991)

*Published by Shambhala Publications

ZEN ESSENCE

The Science of Freedom

Translated & Edited by
THOMAS CLEARY

SHAMBHALA
Boston & London
2000

Shambhala Publications, Inc.
Horticultural Hall
300 Massachusetts Avenue
Boston, MA 02115
www.shambhala.com

ISBN 1-57062-588-3

Printed in the United States of America

Distributed in the United States by Random House, Inc., and in Canada by Random House of Canada Ltd

Library of Congress Cataloging-in-Publication Data

Zen essence: the science of freedom/translated and edited by
Thomas Cleary.
p.   cm.—(Shambhala dragon editions)
Translation of an anthology of the teachings
drawn from the records of the great Chinese Zen
masters from the Tang and Sung dynasties.
ISBN 1-57062-588-3 (pbk.)
1. Zen Buddhism—Doctrines.   I. Cleary,
Thomas F., 1949–
BQ9268.7.Z45   1989   89-42636
294.3′927—dc20   CIP

CONTENTS

ZEN MASTER XUEDOU

ZEN MASTER HUANGLONG

ZEN MASTER YANGQI

ZEN MASTER WUZU

ZEN MASTER FOYAN

TRANSLATOR'S INTRODUCTION

Zen is the essence of Buddhism, freedom is the essence of Zen. At its simplest and most profound level, Zen is purely devoted to liberating the hidden potential of the human mind. The Chinese Zen master Ying-an said, "Zen living is a most direct shortcut, not requiring the exertion of the slightest bit of strength to attain enlightenment and master Zen right where you are."

The freedom that Zen proposes is not remote, but right in this world. It does not require anything extraneous, but can be put into practice in the midst of normal occupations and activities. It is applicable immediately, and develops naturally. Dahui, another great Chinese Zen master, said, "To attain Zen enlightenment it is not necessary to give up family life, quit your job, become a vegetarian, practice asceticism, or flee to a quiet place."

Yet even while effectively *in* the world, Zen freedom is not essentially *of* the world; it is not the same as a freedom that can be instituted or granted by a social or political system. According to Zen teaching, freedom that depends on things of the world can be undermined, and freedom that can be granted can be taken away. Aiming for freedom that cannot be undermined and cannot be taken away, Zen liberation reaches out from within. By its very nature it cannot enter in from outside the individual mind.

Zen liberation is essentially achieved by special knowledge and perception that penetrate the root of experience. This knowledge and perception free the mind from the arbitrary limitations imposed on it by conditioning, thus awakening dormant capacities of consciousness. Dahui explained:

> The realm of the enlightened is not an external realm with manifest characteristics; buddhahood is the realm of the sacred knowledge found in oneself. You do not need paraphernalia, practices, or realizations to attain it. What you need is to clean

out the influences of the psychological afflictions connected with the external world that have been accumulating in your psyche since beginningless time.

Zen cleans the mind for inner perception of its own essential nature; then inner perception of mind's essential purity enables one to remain spontaneously poised and free in all circumstances, so that one may go on clarifying daily experience. The old Japanese Zen master Bunan said,

> People think it is hard to perceive the essential human nature, but in reality it is neither difficult nor easy. Nothing at all can adhere to this essential nature. It is a matter of responding to right and wrong while remaining detached from right and wrong, living in the midst of passions yet being detached from passions, seeing without seeing, hearing without hearing, acting without acting, seeking without seeking.

Enlightened Zen freedom, being in the world yet not of the world, is traditionally likened to a lotus flower, rooted in the mud while blossoming over the water. It is not a negative detachment but a balance of independence and openness. Therefore it is not realized by formal effort but by direct experience and unfolding of the essence of the human mind.

The paradox of Zen freedom is that it is present and available, yet somehow elusive when deliberately sought. It responds to what Bunan called "seeking without seeking." Ying-an put it this way: "Zen has nothing to grab on to. When people who study Zen don't see it, that is because they approach too eagerly."

For this reason, classical Zen books are not manuals of doctrine or ritual to be followed as systematic courses of Zen that are supposed to lead one and all step by step to the inner sanctum. They are written to awaken sleeping dimensions of consciousness, not to inculcate ideas or beliefs.

Countless systems have been devised to approach Zen since the disappearance of the original schools, but none of them is complete or final, and none of them lasts. This is simply the nature of Zen, which speaks to the personal experience of each individual and each time. It is also true of all Buddhist schools, as their scriptures attest. Zen master Dahui said, "If you think there are any verbal formulations that are special mysterious secrets to be transmitted, this is not real Zen."

Zen adds extra dimension to consciousness in both rational and intuitive modes. It does so by deepening and sharpening thought, and by fostering a special kind of insight or knowledge more subtle than thought. Since it is axiomatic that this kind of mental development ultimately cannot be given and cannot be taken, Zen learning needs its own approach.

The essence of the Zen approach is deceptively simple, as explained by the Chinese master Yuanwu: "Set aside all the slogans you have learned and all the intellectual views that stick to your flesh." Zen is the freshest essence of mind, already gone by the time it becomes an idea. The Zen meaning of literature is impact, not ideology.

Because of the very nature of Zen, its essence is neither of the East nor of the West. The classical Zen masters have said that this essence does not belong to any particular culture or philosophy, let alone any particular social class or group. A Zen poet remarked, "On whose door does the moonlight not shine?" It is at the source of ideas, not a product of ideas; and this is what distinguishes the essence of Zen from all derivative philosophy, religion, art, and science.

There are many ways of entering into Zen, and the possibilities that emerge from Zen are even richer. This volume is a collection of hints on realizing and living the essence of Zen, drawn from the works of the greatest Zen masters of ancient China. Translated from the original Chinese records, these unique writings represent the most open and direct forms of instruction in the entire Zen canon. They are not religion or philosophy but a practical psychology of liberation.

This type of Zen literature has been public for centuries and can be enjoyed by anyone. It requires consciousness alone and does not depend on a particular background in Zen Buddhism or any form of Asian culture. It applies directly to the relationship between mind and culture itself, whatever that culture may be. Therefore it relates immediately to the way in which the world is experienced and life is lived, wherever one may be. This is the universal aspect of Zen, the essence of Zen.

Notes on Sources

The translations in this volume are from standard collections in the Zen portion of the Chinese Buddhist canon. The Zen masters quoted lived from the eighth to the fourteenth centuries. Further teachings of some of these masters, especially the earlier ones, are recorded in the translation and appendices of *The Blue Cliff Record* (Boulder, Colo.: Shambhala, 1977). The commentaries in the latter Zen classic are those of Yuanwu, who is also one of the major figures in the literature translated in the present volume.

Virtually all of the famed letters of Dahui, another important teacher in this collection, are in J. C. Cleary's translation *Swampland Flowers* (New York: Grove, 1977). A considerable amount of other material by and about Dahui is also translated in my *Zen Lessons: The Art of Leadership* (Boston: Shambhala, 1989), in which Dahui is known by the epithet Miaoxi. This book also contains more on the teachings of some of the other Zen masters in *Zen Essence*.

ZEN MASTER MAZU

The Normal Mind

The Way does not require cultivation—just don't pollute it.

What is pollution? As long as you have a fluctuating mind fabricating artificialities and contrivances, all of this is pollution.

If you want to understand the Way directly, the normal mind is the Way.

What I mean by the normal mind is the mind without artificiality, without subjective judgments, without grasping or rejection.

The Root

The founders of Zen said that one's own essence is inherently complete. Just don't linger over good or bad things—that is called practice of the Way. To grasp the good and reject the bad, to contemplate emptiness and enter concentration, is all in the province of contrivance—and if you go on seeking externals, you get further and further estranged.

Just end the mental objectivization of the world. A single thought of the wandering mind is the root of birth and death in the world. Just don't have a single thought and you'll get rid of the root of birth and death.

The Oceanic Reflection

Human delusions of time immemorial, deceit, pride, deviousness, and conceit, have conglomerated into one body. That is why scripture says that this body is just made of elements, and its appearance and disappearance is just that of elements, which have no identity. When successive thoughts do not await one another, and each thought dies peacefully away, this is called absorption in the oceanic reflection.

Delusion and Enlightenment

Delusion means you are not aware of your own fundamental mind; enlightenment means you realize your own fundamental essence. Once enlightened, you do not become deluded anymore.

If you understand mind and objects, then false conceptions do not arise; when false conceptions do not arise, this is acceptance of the beginninglessness of things. You have always had it, and you have it now—there is no need to cultivate the Way and sit in meditation.

ZEN MASTER DAZHU

Artificial Zen

You are luckily all right by yourself, yet you struggle artificially. Why do you want to put on fetters and go to prison? You are busy every day claiming to study Zen, learn the Way, and interpret Buddhism, but this alienates you even further. It is just chasing sound and form. When will you ever stop?

Your Treasure

My teacher said to me, "The treasure house within you contains everything, and you are free to use it. You don't need to seek outside."

ZEN MASTER LINJI

True Perception and Understanding

People who study Buddhism should seek real, true perception and understanding for now. If you attain real, true perception and understanding, birth and death don't affect you—you are free to go or stay. You needn't seek wonders, for wonders come of themselves.

Self-confidence

What I point out to you is only that you shouldn't allow yourselves to be confused by others. Act when you need to, without further hesitation or doubt.

People today can't do this—what is their affliction? Their affliction is in their lack of self-confidence.

If you do not spontaneously trust yourself sufficiently, you will be in a frantic state, pursuing all sorts of objects and being changed by those objects, unable to be independent.

Buddha Within

There is no stability in the world; it is like a house on fire. This is not a place where you can stay for a long time. The murderous demon of impermanence is instantaneous, and it does not choose between the upper and lower classes, or between the old and the young.

If you want to be no different from the buddhas and Zen masters, just don't seek externally.

The pure light in a moment of awareness in your mind is the Buddha's essence within you. The nondiscriminating light in a moment of awareness in your mind is the Buddha's wisdom within you. The undifferentiated light in a moment of awareness in your mind is the Buddha's manifestation within you.

No Obsessions

It is most urgent that you seek real, true perception and under standing, so you can be free in the world and not be confused by ordinary spiritualists.

It is best to have no obsessions. Just don't be contrived. Simply be normal.

You impulsively seek elsewhere, looking to others for your own hands and feet. This is already mistaken.

The Mind Ground

The mind ground can go into the ordinary, into the holy, into the pure, into the defiled, into the real, into the conventional; but it is not your "real" or "conventional," "ordinary" or "holy." It can put labels on all the real and conventional, the ordinary and holy, but the real and conventional, the ordinary and holy, cannot put labels on someone in the mind ground. If you can get it, use it, without putting any more labels on it.

Understanding People

When followers of Zen come to see me, I have already understood them completely. How can I do this? Simply because my perception is independent—externally I do not grasp the ordinary or the holy, internally I do not dwell on the fundamental. I see all the way through and do not doubt or err anymore.

Autonomy

Just be autonomous wherever you are, and right there is realization. Situations that come up cannot change you. Even if you have bad habits, you will spontaneously be liberated from them.

Spiritual Dilettantes

Zen students today are totally unaware of truth. They are like foraging goats that pick up whatever they bump into. They do not distinguish between the servant and the master, or between the guest and the host.

People like this enter Zen with distorted minds, and are unable to enter effectively into dynamic situations. They may be called true initiates, but actually they are really mundane people.

Those who really leave attachments must master real, true perception to distinguish the enlightened from the obsessed, the genuine from the artificial, the unregenerate from the sage.

If you can make these discernments, you can be said to have really left dependency.

Professional Buddhist clergy who cannot tell obsession from enlightenment have just left one social group and entered another social group. They cannot really be said to be independent.

Now there is an obsession with Buddhism that is mixed in with the real thing. Those with clear eyes cut through both obsession and Buddhism. If you love the sacred and despise the ordinary, you are still bobbing in the ocean of delusion.

Labels and Objective Truth

Because you grasp labels and slogans, you are hindered by those labels and slogans, both those used in ordinary life and those considered sacred. Thus they obstruct your perception of objective truth, and you cannot understand clearly.

The Free Self

If you want to be free, get to know your real self. It has no form, no appearance, no root, no basis, no abode, but is lively and buoyant. It responds with versatile facility, but its function cannot be located. Therefore when you look for it you become further from it, when you seek it you turn away from it all the more.

No Concern

Just put thoughts to rest and don't seek outwardly anymore. When things come up, then give them your attention; just trust what is functional in you at present, and you have nothing to be concerned about.

Blind Baldies

There are blind baldies who, after they have eaten their fill, do zazen and practice meditation, arresting thoughts leaking out to prevent them from arising, shunning clamor and seeking quiet. This is a deviated form of Zen.

Uncritical Acceptance

You take the words of these ordinary Zen teachers for the real Way, supposing that Zen teachers are incomprehensible and as an ordinary person you dare not attempt to assess those old timers. You are blind if you take this view all your life, contrary to the evidence of your own two eyes.

Tourist Traps

At Zen centers they say there is a Way to be practiced and a religious truth to be realized. Tell me, what religious truth is realized, what way is practiced? In your present functioning, what do you lack? What would you fix?

Younger newcomers, not understanding this, immediately believe these mesmerists and let them talk about things that tie people up.

Supernormal Faculties

The six supernormal faculties of the enlightened are the ability to enter the realm of form without being confused by form, to enter the realm of sound without being confused by sound, to enter the realm of scent without being confused by scent, to enter the realm of flavor without being confused by flavor, to enter the realm of feeling without being confused by feeling, to enter the realm of phenomena without being confused by phenomena.

Objective Perception and Understanding

If you want to perceive and understand objectively, just don't allow yourself to be confused by people. Detach from whatever you find inside or outside yourself—detach from religion, tradition, and society, and only then will you attain liberation. When you are not entangled in things, you pass through freely to autonomy.

Zen Teaching

I have no doctrine to give people—I just cure ailments and unlock fetters.

Adding Mud to Dirt

There are Zen students who are in chains when they go to a teacher, and the teacher adds another chain. The students are delighted, unable to discern one thing from another. This is called a guest looking at a guest.

Slavery

When I say there is nothing outside, students who do not understand me interpret this in terms of inwardness, so they sit silent and still, taking this to be Zen Buddhism.

This is a big mistake. If you take a state of unmoving clarity to be Zen, you are recognizing ignorance as a slave master.

Movement and Stillness

If you try to grasp Zen in movement, it goes into stillness. If you try to grasp Zen in stillness, it goes into movement. It is like a fish hidden in a spring, drumming up waves and dancing independently.

Movement and stillness are two states. The Zen master, who does not depend on anything, makes deliberate use of both movement and stillness.

ZEN MASTER YANGSHAN

Zen Teaching

There is interaction if there is a call for it, no interaction if there is no call for it.

Deep and Shallow

If I were to explain the source of Zen, there wouldn't be a single person around, let alone a group of five hundred or seven hundred. If I talk about this and that, however, you race forward to pick it up. This is like fooling a child with an empty fist—there is no reality in it.

The Zen Essence

I explain to you matters pertaining to enlightenment, but don't try to keep your mind on them. Just turn to the ocean of your own essence and develop practical accord with its true nature.

Supernormal Capacities

You do not need supernormal capacities, because these are outgrowths of enlightenment. For now you need to know the mind and get to its source.

Root and Branches

Just get the root, don't worry about the branches, for someday you will come to have them naturally. If you have not attained the basis, even if you consciously study you cannot attain the outgrowths either.

The Inner Gaze

You should turn your attention within—don't memorize my words. You have been turning from light to darkness since before you can remember, so the roots of your subjective ideas are deep and hard to uproot all at once. This is why I temporarily use expedients to take away your coarse perceptions.

ZEN MASTER FAYAN

False Zen Teachers

It is wrong to act as a teacher of others before your own mind ground is clearly illumined.

The Basis of Zen

The teaching of the mind ground is the basis of Zen study. The mind ground is the great awareness of being as is.

Confusion

Due to confusion, people mistake things for themselves; covetousness flares up, and they get into vicious cycles that cloud perceptions and enshroud them in ignorance. The vicious cycles go on and on, and people cannot be free.

The Deterioration of Zen

The purpose of Zen is to enable people to immediately transcend the ordinary and the holy, just getting people to awaken on their own, forever cutting off the root of doubt.

Many people in modern times disregard this. They may join Zen groups, but they are lazy about Zen study. Even if they achieve concentration, they do not choose real teachers. Through the errors of false teachers, they likewise lose the way.

Without having understood senses and objects, as soon as they possess themselves of some false interpretation they become obsessed by it and lose the correct basis completely.

They are only interested in becoming leaders and being known as teachers. While they value an empty reputation in the world, they bring ill on themselves. Not only do they make their successors blind and deaf, they also cause the influence of Zen to degenerate.

Sectarianism

Zen is not founded or sustained on the premise that there is a doctrine to be transmitted. It is just a matter of direct guidance to the human mind, perception of its essence, and achievement of awakening. How could there be any sectarian styles to be valued?

There were differences in the modes of teaching set up by later Zen teachers, and there were both tradition and change. The methods employed by a number of famous Zen masters came to be continued as traditions, to the point where their descendants became sectarians and did not get to the original reality. Eventually they made many digressions, contradicting and attacking each other. They do not distinguish the profound from the superficial, and do not know that the Great Way has no sides and the streams of truth have the same flavor.

Discernment

Zen teachers need first to distinguish false and true, then they must clearly understand the time.

Degenerate Zen

Zen teachers in recent times have lost the basis, so students have no way to learn. There is egotistical contention, and impermanent states are taken to be attainments.

Principle and Fact

Zen Buddhism includes both principle and fact. Fact is based on principle, principle is illustrated by fact. Principle and fact work together like eyes and feet.

Subjective Judgments

If you make subjective, personalistic judgments of past and present events, not having been through the process of refining and purifying your insight, this is like trying to do a sword dance without having learned to handle a sword.

Understanding and Imagination

It is not possible to fathom the intention of the words or acts of the enlightened by indulging in fantasy.

Zen Succession

If you memorize slogans, you are unable to make subtle adaptations according to the situation. It is not that there is no way to teach insight to learners, but once you have learned a way, it is essential that you get it to work completely. If you just stick to your teacher's school and memorize slogans, this is not enlightenment, it is a part of intellectual knowledge.

This is why it is said, "When your perception only equals that of your teacher, you lessen the teacher's virtue by half. When your perception goes beyond the teacher, only then can you express the teacher's teaching."

The sixth ancestor of Zen said to someone who had just been awakened, "What I tell you is not a secret. The secret is in you."

Another Zen master said to a companion, "Everything flows from your own heart."

ZEN MASTER FENYANG

The Work of a Teacher

Someone asked Fenyang, "What is the work of a teaching master?" Fenyang replied, "Impersonally guiding those with affinity."

Moon and Clouds

The original Buddha-nature of all living beings is like the bright moon in the sky—it is only because it is covered by floating clouds that it cannot appear.

Independent Knowing

You should know by yourself what is holy and what is ordinary, what is wrong and what is right—don't be concerned with others' judgments. How many people have ever managed to find out every subtlety? People arbitrarily follow material senses, running like idiots.

Time and Time Out

When will you ever stop competing? Before you realize, the scenery of spring has turned to autumn. The leaves fall, the geese migrate, the frost gradually grows colder. Clothed and shod, what more do you seek?

Devil, Buddha, and Mind

When you know the mind, mind is Buddha. If you don't know it, it is the devil. Devil and Buddha are products of one mind. Buddha is real, the devil is madnesss.

Direct Pointing to Basic Mind

Few people believe their inherent mind is Buddha. Most will not take this seriously, and therefore are cramped. They are wrapped up in illusions, cravings, resentments, and other afflictions, all because they love the cave of ignorance.

Sudden Awakening

When you suddenly realize the source of mind, you open a box of jewels. Honorable on earth and in the heavens, you are aloof even from the joy of meditation. The essence containing all flavors is the supreme delicacy, worth more than ten thousand ounces of pure gold.

Communication through the Source

When you are deluded and full of doubt, even a thousand books of scripture are still not enough. When you have realized understanding, even one word is already too much.

Zen is communicated personally, through mental recognition. It is not handed on directly by written words.

Summary of Zen Practice

When you're settled in Zen, your mind is serene, unaffected by worldly distractions. You enter the realm of enlightenment, and transcend the ordinary world, leaving the world while in the midst of society.

Realizing the Way

Once you realize universal emptiness, all situations are naturally mastered. You have perfect communion with what is beyond the world, while embracing what is within all realms of being.

If you miss the essence of Zen, after all there's nothing to it. If you get its function, it has spiritual effect.

The real Way of "nonminding" is not a school for petty people.

ZEN MASTER XUEDOU

The Living Meaning of Zen

Someone asked Xuedou, "What is the living meaning of Zen?"
Xuedou said, "The mountains are high, the oceans are wide."

Where Do You Get It?

Someone asked Xuedou, "As it is said, 'The one road beyond is
not transmitted by any of the sages.' Where did you get it?"
Xuedou said, "I thought you were a Zen practitioner."

An Eye-Opening Experience

Where the sword wheel flies, sun and moon lose their shine;
when the jewel staff strikes, heaven and earth lose their color. Through
this experience, all devils' guts burst; through this experience, all
sages' eyes open.

Illuminating Perception

When you illuminate your perception, your eyes are like a
thousand suns, so that nothing can escape notice. Ordinarily, people
just have never been so observant, but they should not give up in
frustration because of underestimating themselves.

Truth and Wisdom

The wise boldly pick up a truth as soon as they hear it. Don't
wait for a moment, or you'll lose your head.

Zen Teaching

Someone asked Xuedou, "What is your manner of teaching?"
Xuedou replied, "When guests come, one should see them."

Spoiling the Broth

Once there was a Zen elder who didn't talk to his group at all during a retreat. One of the group said, "This way, I've wasted the whole retreat. I don't expect the teacher to explain Buddhism; it would be enough to hear the two words 'Absolute Truth.' "

The elder heard of this and said, "Don't be so quick to complain. There's not even a single word to say about 'Absolute Truth.' " Then when he had said this, he gnashed his teeth and said, "It was pointless to say that."

In the next room was another elder who overheard this and said, "A fine pot of soup, befouled by two rat droppings."

Whose pot hasn't one or two droppings in it?

The Zen River

The river of Zen is quiet, even in the waves; the water of stability is clear, even in the waves.

ZEN MASTER HUANGLONG

Teacherless Knowledge

The universal body of reality is so subtle that you do not hear it when you deliberately listen for it, and you do not see it when you look at it. As for the pure knowledge that has no teacher, how can it be attained by thought or study?

Open Your Eyes

Seekers should open their own eyes—don't let yourselves in for regret later on. Zen cannot be reached by psychic powers or by cultivation of special experiences. Zen cannot be discussed by means of the knowledge or intelligence of the merely learned.

Knowledge and Feelings

The basis of sentient existence is the ocean of knowledge, which is its source. The substance of the flow of conscious existence is the body of Reality.

But when feelings arise, knowledge is blocked, so true reality is unknown in everyday life. As mental images change, things differ, with people tending toward objects of habit and not returning.

The Zen Way

The Way does not need cultivation—just don't defile it. Zen does not need study—the important thing is stopping the mind.

When the mind is stopped, there is no rumination. Because it is not cultivated, you walk on the Way at every step.

When there is no rumination, there is no world to transcend. Because it is not cultivated, there is no Way to seek.

Seeking

To travel around to various schools looking for teachers is outward seeking. To take the inherent nature of awareness as the ocean and the silent knowledge of transcendent wisdom as Zen, is called inward seeking.

To seek outwardly busies you fatally; to seek inwardly while dwelling on mind and body binds you fatally.

Therefore Zen is neither inward nor outward, not being or nonbeing, not real or false. As it is said, "Inner and outer views are both wrong."

Leavings

"When ordinary and sacred feelings are forgotten, Being is revealed, real and eternal. Just detach from arbitrary involvements, and you awaken to Being as it is."

Although these are the leavings of an ancient Zen master, there are many people who cannot partake of them. I've lost considerable profit just by bringing them up.

Can anyone discern? If you can, you will recognize the disease of "Buddhism" and the disease of "Zen."

Living Zen

To drink up the ocean and turn a mountain upside down is an ordinary affair for a Zennist. Zen seekers should sit on the site of universal enlightenment right in the midst of all the thorny situations in life, and recognize their original face while mixing with the ordinary world.

Real Detachment

"Where people of today dwell, I do not dwell. What people of today do, I do not do." If you clearly understand what this really means, you must be able to enter a pit of fire with your whole body.

Golden Chains

Someone asked Huanglong, "It is said that someone who is uncontrived and unconcerned is still hindered by golden chains—what is wrong?"

Huanglong said, "When a word enters the public domain, it can't be withdrawn for nine years."

In and Out

All sages since remote antiquity have entered the pit of life and death, gone into the fire of ignorance, to help people out. What about you? How do you enter?

If people can enter, this can be called not burning in fire, not drowning in water.

If people cannot enter, they not only cannot help themselves, they cannot help others.

ZEN MASTER YANGQI

Lost and Found

When body and mind are pure, all things are pure. When all things are pure, body and mind are pure.

"The coin lost in the river is to be retrieved from the river."

Still Worldly

When you detach from the whole universe, everywhere is dark. When you let go of the absolute, the rain is seasonal and the breeze is moderate. Even so, there is still worldliness there.

The Ancient Teaching

Someone asked Yangqi, "As it is said, 'If you want to escape from clamor in the mind, you should read the ancient teaching.' What is the ancient teaching?"

Yangqi replied, "The moon is bright in space, the waves are calm on the ocean."

The inquirer asked, "How does one read it?"

Yangqi said, "Watch your step."

The Supreme Vehicle of Zen

I am asked to expound the supreme vehicle of Zen, but if it is the supreme vehicle, even the sages stand aside, buddhas and Zen masters disappear.

Why? Because you are all the same as the buddhas of old.

But can you really believe and trust this?
If you really can, let us all disband and go our separate ways.
If you don't leave, I'll go on fooling you.

Mind and Phenomena

Mind is the faculty, phenomena are the data: both are like scratches in a mirror.

When there are no scratches or dust, the clarity of the mirror shows.

When mind and phenomena are both forgotten, then your nature is real.

Silent Zen

Someone asked Yangqi, "When the founder of Zen came from India to China, he sat facing a wall for nine years—what does this mean?"

Yangqi said, "As an Indian, he couldn't speak Chinese."

ZEN MASTER WUZU

Zen Teaching

To be a Zen teacher, it is imperative to "drive away the plow-man's ox, snatch away the hungry man's food."

When you drive away the plowman's ox, that makes his crops abundant; when you snatch away the hungry man's food, that frees him from hunger forever.

For most people that hear this saying, it is like the wind passing the ears. If you drive away the plowman's ox, how does that make his crops abundant? If you snatch away the hungry man's food, how does that free him from hunger?

At this point, you must have the ability to drive away the plowman's ox and snatch away the hungry man's food, then give a pressing thrust, causing people to reach their wit's end. Then you tell them, "Blessings are not received twice, calamities do not occur alone."

Something Indescribable

There is something in the world that is neither in the sphere of the ordinary nor in the sphere of the holy. It is neither in the realm of the false nor in the realm of the true.

Halcyon

When there is not a speck of cloud dotting the great clarity for ten thousand miles, sun and moon in the original sky are of themselves clear.

It is not permitted for a general to see great peace, but a general may establish great peace.

The Goal of Zen

To study Zen, first you must obtain directions to the ultimate goal. Hearing sound and seeing form are inconceivable. From the eternal sky every night the moon shines on every home; its reflection descends into a quiet pool, but how many know?

Seeking without Finding

Few seekers of Zen attain it. When will judgments ever cease? If you talk about high and low based on words, that is like before enlightenment.

Everyone Can Arrive

There is a road to emptiness by which everyone can arrive. Those who do arrive realize that its rich flavor is lasting. The ground of mind doesn't produce useless plants; naturally the body radiates light.

Talking about Zen

Talking about Zen all the time is like looking for fish tracks in a dry riverbed.

ZEN MASTER YUANWU

The Aim of Zen

When enlightened Zen masters set up teachings for a spiritual path, the only concern is to clarify the mind to arrive at its source. It is complete in everyone, yet people turn away from this basic mind because of their illusions.

Immediate Zen

If you have developed great capacity and cutting insight, you can undertake Zen right where you are. Without getting it from another, you understand clearly on your own.

The penetrating spiritual light and vast open tranquility have never been interrupted since beginningless time. The pure, uncontrived, ineffable, complete true mind does not act as a partner to objects of material sense, and is not a companion of myriad things.

When the mind is always as clear and bright as ten suns shining together, detached from views and beyond feelings, cutting through the ephemeral illusions of birth and death, this is what is meant by the saying, "Mind itself is Buddha."

Intellectual Egotists

Many worldly intellectuals just study Zen for something to talk about, something that will enhance their reputation. They consider this a lofty interest, and try to use it to assert superiority over others. This just increases their egotism.

Motivation

When your original reason for studying Zen is not right, you wind up having labored without accomplishment. This is why ancients used to urge people to study Zen as if they were on the brink of death.

Peace

Human lives go along with circumstances. It is not necessary to reject activity and seek quiet; just make yourself inwardly empty while outwardly harmonious. Then you will be at peace in the midst of frenetic activity in the world.

Instant Zen

In Zen, it is not difficult for those of keen faculties and higher insight to attain a thousand understandings at one hearing.

Firm Footing

It is necessary for your footing to be firm and solid, accurate and sure. Taking control and being the master, you become one with all different situations, like space without barriers. When profound, open clarity has no change, and is consistent at all times, only then can you be at peace.

Changing Methods

Zen teachers of true vision and great liberation have made changes in method along the way, to prevent people from sticking to names and forms and falling into rationalizations.

The Purpose of Zen

Over the course of centuries, Zen has branched out into different schools with individual methods, but the purpose is still the same—to point directly to the human mind.

Once the ground of mind is clarified, there is no obstruction at all—you shed views and interpretations that are based on concepts such as victory and defeat, self and others, right and wrong.

Thus you pass through all that and reach a realm of great rest and tranquility.

Opening the Mind

Zen requires opening the mind and losing all false cognition and false views. When nothing hangs on your mind and you have passed through cleanly, then you are ready for refinement.

Buddha's Teachings

When a buddha appears in the world and expounds various teachings according to people's inclinations, all of the teachings are expedients, just for the purpose of breaking through obsessions, doubts, intellectual interpretations, and egocentric ideas.

If there were no such false consciousness and false views, there would be no need for buddhas to appear and expound so many teachings.

Release

In Zen, sudden release into realization isn't subject to either ruin or support by other people. Be totally aloof, and one day you will boldly pass through with penetrating senses to experience Zen directly.

Then you use it at will, you act at will, without so many things going through your mind.

When this is developed to maturity and you let go all at once, you immediately attain rest and comfort right where you are.

Half-Baked Zen

What is most difficult to rectify is half-baked Zen, where you stick to quiet stillness and consider this the ultimate treasure, keeping it in your heart, radiantly aware of it all the time, carrying around a bunch of mixed-up knowledge and understanding, claiming to have vision and to have attained the approval of a Zen master, just increasing your egoism.

Zen Mind

In those who attain Zen, mental machinations disappear, vision and action are forgotten, and there are no subjective views.

Zen adepts just remain free, and are imperceptible to anyone, either would-be supporters or would-be antagonists.

They walk on the bottom of the deepest ocean, uncontaminated, with free minds, acting normally, indistinguishable from the average person.

Though they liberate their minds directly and develop to this state, they still are unwilling to dwell here.

They sense the slightest thing as mountainous; anything that seems to cause obstruction they immediately push away.

Although this is purely the ground of noumenon, there is still nothing in it to grasp. If you grasp it, it becomes a sticky view.

Therefore it is said, "The Tao is mindless of union with humanity; when people are unminding, they unite with the Tao."

How could anyone show off and claim to have attained Zen?

Living and Dead Words

Study the living word of Zen, not the dead word. When you attain understanding of the living word, you never forget it. When you attain understanding of the dead word, you can't even save yourself.

The Sword of Death, the Sword of Life

It is said that you need the sword that kills in order to kill, and you need the sword that gives life in order to give life.

Once people have been killed, they should be brought to life, and once they have been brought to life they should be killed.

If either type of technique is used in isolation, there is an imbalance.

Don't Seek Zen

If you want to attain intimate realization of Zen, first of all don't seek it. What is attained by seeking has already fallen into intellection.

The great treasury of Zen has always been open and clear; it has always been the source of power for all your actions.

But only when you stop your compulsive mind, to reach the point where not a single thing is born, do you pass through to freedom, not falling into feelings and not dwelling on concepts, transcending all completely.

Then Zen is obvious everywhere in the world, with the totality of everything everywhere turning into its great function.

Everything comes from your own heart. This is what one ancient called bringing out the family treasure.

Direct Experience of Zen

Zen originally is not established on slogans, it just points directly to the human mind.

Direct pointing is just pointing to that which is inherent in everyone, though in a shell of unawareness.

When the whole being appears responsively, it is no different from that of the sages since antiquity.

This is what is called the originally pure subtle luminosity of naturally real essence, which swallows and spits out the whole universe, individually freed from the material senses.

Only by detaching from thoughts and cutting off feelings, utterly transcending ordinary parameters, with great perceptivity and great insight, using inherent power, can this be directly experienced in your present situation.

Zen Attainment

An ancient master said, "Those who have attained Zen just keep free, desireless and independent all the time."

Zen Practice

Just still the thoughts in your mind. It is good to do this right in the midst of disturbance. When you are working on this, penetrate the heights and the depths.

Liberation

Let go of all your previous imaginings, opinions, interpretations, worldly knowledge, intellectualism, egoism, and competitiveness; become like a dead tree, like cold ashes. When you reach the point where feelings are ended, views are gone, and your mind is clean and naked, you open up to Zen realization.

After that it is also necessary to develop consistency, keeping the mind pure and free from adulteration at all times. If there is the slightest fluctuation, there is no hope of transcending the world.

Cut through resolutely, and then your state will be peaceful. When you cannot be included in any stage, whether of sages or of ordinary people, then you are like a bird freed from its cage.

Resolve

The Way is arrived at by enlightenment. The first priority is to establish resolve—it is no small matter to step directly from the bondage of the ordinary person into transcendent experience of the realm of sages. It requires that your mind be firm as steel to cut off the flow of birth and death, accept your original real nature, not see anything at all as existing inside or outside yourself, and make your heart perfectly clear, without any obstruction, so all actions and endeavors emerge from the fundamental.

The Essential Point

The essential point in learning Zen is to make the roots deep and the stem firm. Twenty-four hours a day, be aware of where you are and what you do.

When no thoughts have arisen and nothing at all is on your mind, you merge with the boundless and become wholly empty and still. Then your actions are not interrupted by doubt and hesitation.

This is called the fundamental matter right at hand.

As soon as you produce any opinion or interpretation, and want to attain Zen and be a master, you have already fallen into psychological and material realms. You have become trapped by ordinary senses and perceptions, by ideas of gain and loss, by ideas of right and wrong. Half drunk and half sober, you cannot manage effectively.

Don't Linger

As soon as you sense any lingering or obstruction, all of it is false imagining. Just make your mind clean and free, like space, like a mirror, like the sun in the sky.

Autonomy and Integration

When you are free and independent, you are not bound by anything, so you do not seek liberation. Consummating the process of Zen, you become unified. Then there are no mundane things outside of Buddhism, and there is no Buddhism outside of mundane things.

Consulting Teachers

Step back on your own to look into reality long enough to attain an unequivocally true and real experience of enlightenment. Then with every thought you are consulting infinite teachers.

Substance and Function

Complete, tranquil, open, still—such is the substance of the Way. Expanding, contracting, killing, giving life—such is its subtle function.

Extremes

If you haven't attained clear true vision, this causes you to lapse into extremes, so that you lose contact with reality.

Tools

The words of buddhas and Zen masters are just tools, means of gaining access to truth. Once you are clearly enlightened and experience truth, all the teachings are within you.

Then you look upon the verbal teachings of buddhas and Zen masters as something in the realm of reflections or echoes, and you do not wear them around on your head.

Misuse of Tools

Nowadays many Zen students do not go to the root of the design of Zen, instead they just try to pick out sayings and discuss them in terms of familiarity and strangeness, of winning and losing. They interpret the ephemeral as being real.

Snowflakes on a Furnace

You should refrain from dependence on anything at all, pure or impure. Then mindfulness and mindlessness, views and no view, will be like a snowflake on a red-hot furnace.

Nonminding

When you are inwardly empty and quiet, while outwardly detached from perception, you naturally attain penetrating experience of nonminding, which means that even if everything happens at once, that cannot disturb your spirit, and even though all kinds of troubles face you, that does not affect your thoughts.

Serene Response

When you can actively respond to changes in the midst of the hurly-burly of life while being inwardly empty and serene, and can also avoid infatuation with quietude when in a quiet environment, then wherever you are is where you live. Only those who have attained the fundamental are capable of being inwardly empty while outwardly harmonious.

Zen Life and Death

The capacity of speech is not only in the tongue, the ability to talk is not just a matter of words.

The enlightened know that spoken words are not to be relied on, so the sayings of the ancient Zen masters are only intended to induce people to directly witness the nexus of causes and conditions that constitute what has always been of greatest concern.

Therefore the teachings of the Buddhist scriptures are like fingers pointing to the moon. When you know this matter of greatest concern, then you stop formal study and apply this knowledge thoroughly, using it with comprehensive penetration.

Eventually you will reach the point of immovability, where you can pick up Zen and use it, putting it away and letting it out expertly.

Then you can see through ordinary situations and detach from them without leaving a trace.

And when you come to the border of life and death, when they interlock but do not mix, you depart serenely, unperturbed. This is the Zen of facing death.

Zen Teachers

Zen teachers should be compassionate, gentle, and skilled at adaptation, dealing with people impartially, minding their own business and not contending with anyone.

Dealing with Opposition

If people find fault with you and try to put you in a bad light, wrongly slandering and vilifying you, just step back and observe yourself. Don't harbor any dislike, don't enter into any contests, and don't get upset, angry, or resentful.

Just cut right through it and be as if you never heard or saw it. Eventually malevolent pests will disappear of themselves.

If you contend with them, then a bad name will bounce back and forth with never an end in sight.

Zen Enlightenment and Zen Work

An ancient Zen master said that Zen is like learning archery; only after long practice do you hit the bullseye.

Enlightenment is experienced instantaneously, but Zen work must be done over a long time, like a bird that when first hatched is naked and scrawny, but then grows feathers as it is nourished, until it can fly high and far.

Therefore those who have attained clear penetrating enlightenment then need fine tuning.

When it comes to worldly situations, by which ordinary people get suffocated, those who have attained Zen get through them all by being empty. Thus everything is their own gateway to liberation.

False Zen Teachers

Zen teachers without the methodology of real experts unavoidably cheat and deceive those whom they try to teach, leading them into confusion, fooling around with a bunch of curios.

Zen Devices

The intention of all Zen devices, states, sayings, and expressions is in their ability to hook the seeker. The only important thing is liberation—people should not be attached to the means.

Cliché

Although the great Zen teachers did not establish clichés and slogans, eventually seekers misapprehended this and turned this itself into a cliché and a slogan—they made a cliché of no cliché, and a slogan of no slogan. They should not cling to the means as an end.

Perception and Response

Unless your heart is open and serene, with nothing touching your feelings, how can you respond completely without error and perceive things before they begin to act?

Essential Nature and Ultimate Truth

Zen study requires you to see your essential nature and understand ultimate truth.

Immediately forget feelings and detach from perceptions, so your heart is clear and your mind is simple, not comparing gain and loss, not making a contest of better and worse.

Unconcern

Cut through all situations and don't allow yourself to continue with thoughts of whether these situations are favorable or adverse. Eventually you will naturally reach the realm of nondoing and unconcern. But if you have the slightest desire for unconcern, this has already become a concern.

Pride

If you have the idea of superiority and are proud of your ability, this is a disaster.

Concepts and Training

To study Zen conceptually is like drilling in ice for fire, like digging a hole to look for the sky. It just increases mental fatigue. To study Zen by training is adding mud to dirt, scattering sand in the eyes, impeding you more and more.

Penetrating Zen

People who are sharp should have their feet on the ground, and need an iron spine, traveling through the world looking on everything as illusory, holding still and being the master, not following human sentiments, cutting through discrimination between others and self, and getting rid of intellectual interpretations of Zen.

Then, when it comes to practical function, responding to conditions, they don't fall into clichés. Developing single-minded persistence, keeping profound calm, lightening body and mind, while in the midst of the toil of the world they penetrate through to freedom.

Trust and Insight

If you can give up your former knowledge and understanding, thus making your heart open, not keeping anything at all on your mind, so you experience a clear empty solidity where speech and thought do not apply, you will directly merge with the fundamental source, sinking into the infinite, spontaneously attaining inherent wisdom that has no attainment.

This is called thorough trust and penetrating insight. There is, moreover, still boundless, fathomless, measureless great potential and great function yet to be realized.

Stumbled Past

As soon as you try to chase and grab Zen, you've already stumbled past it.

Zen Experience

Set aside all the slogans you have learned and all the intellectual views that stick to your skin and cling to your flesh. Make your mind empty, not manifesting any thoughts on your own, not doing anything at all. Then you can attain thoroughgoing Zen experience.

But even when you reach this point, you should still realize that there is progressive action that transcends a teacher.

Direct Zen

If you have great perceptions and capacities, you need not necessarily contemplate the sayings and stories of ancient Zen masters. Just correct your attention and quiet your mind from the time you arise in the morning, and whatever you say or do, review it carefully and see where it comes from and what makes all this happen.

Once you can pass through right in the midst of present worldly conditions, the same applies to all conditions—what need is there to remove them?

Then you can go beyond "Zen," transcend all parameters, and magically produce a sanctuary of purity, effortlessness, and coolness, right in the midst of the turmoil of the world.

Nondualism

You do not have to abandon worldly activities in order to attain effortless unconcern. You should know that worldly activities and effortless unconcern are not two different things—but if you keep thinking about rejection and grasping, you make them into two.

Nonabiding

A scripture says, "All things are established on a nonabiding basis."

Another scripture says, "Activate the mind without dwelling on anything."

An ancient Zen master said, "Don't mind anything or dwell on anything, whether of the world or beyond the world."

If you dwell on anything, you get stuck, and cannot change effectively.

Subjective Zen

Many intelligent people understand Zen subjectively, and are unable to let go of their subjectivity. They still their minds without experiencing their real nature, and think this is emptiness. They try to abandon existence to cling to emptiness. This is a serious malady.

Dissolving Illusions

It is necessary to detach from both rejection and clinging, from both being and nonbeing, so that you are unburdened, completely tranquil, empty and still, calm and peaceful.

Then you can trust this true pure ineffable mind, and when mundane conditions beckon involvement, you notice it doesn't go along with them.

You can only do this by long-term work on your own, empty and free, to dissolve away illusions and bring about your own insight.

Basic Mind

When you are aware of the completeness, fluidity, and boundlessness of the basic mind, how can sense objects be partners to it? Basic mind is utterly free, open and pure, clear and ethereal; keep thoroughly aware of it, and do not allow superficiality. Then it is so high there is nothing above it, so broad it is boundless; clean and bare, perfectly round, this basic mind is without contamination or contrivance.

ZEN MASTER FOYAN

Saving Energy

Zen practice requires detachment from thought. This is the best way to save energy. Just detach from emotional thought and understand that there is no objective world. Then you will know how to practice Zen.

Mind and World

Once there was a monk who specialized in the Buddhist precepts, and had kept to them all his life. Once when he was walking at night, he stepped on something. It made a squishing sound, and he imagined he had stepped on an egg-bearing frog. This caused him no end of alarm and regret, in view of the Buddhist precept against taking life, and when he finally went to sleep that night he dreamed that hundreds of frogs came to him demanding his life.

The monk was terribly upset, but when morning came he looked and found that what he had stepped on was an overripe eggplant. At that moment his feeling of uncertainty suddenly stopped, and for the first time he realized the meaning of the saying that there is no objective world. Then he finally knew how to practice Zen.

Inherent Zen

Why do you not understand your nature, when it is inherently there? There is not much to Buddhism—it just requires getting to the essential.

We do not teach you to annihilate random thoughts, suppress

body and mind, shut your eyes, and say this is Zen. Zen is not like this.

You should observe your present state—what is the reason for it? Why do you become confused?

Discrimination and Nondiscrimination

You should become aware of the nondiscriminating mind without leaving the discriminating mind; become aware of that which has no perception without leaving perception.

Independence

What do you go to a "Zen center" for? You should make a living on your own, and not listen to what others say.

Who Is It?

Search back into your own vision—think back to the mind that thinks. Who is it?

Mind's Eye

It is as though you have an eye that sees all forms but does not see itself—this is how your mind is. Its light penetrates everywhere and engulfs everything, so why does it not know itself?

Rationalizations

As soon as you rationalize, it is hard to understand Zen. You will have to stop rationalizing before you will get it.

Some people hear this kind of talk and say there is nothing to say and no reason—they do not realize they are already rationalizing when they do this.

Going in Circles

Why do you not understand your mind? First you make "your own mind" into a cliché, then you use your mind to seek its realization. This is called driving a spike into a stump and then running in circles around the stump.

Recognition

Zen enlightenment is as if you have been away from home for many years, when you suddenly see your father in town. You know him right away, without a doubt. There is no need to ask anyone else whether he is your father or not.

Zen Perception

You can be called a Zen student only when you perceive before signs appear, before falling into thought, before ideas sprout.

Stepping Back

You should step back and investigate. How do you step back? It is not a matter of sitting there ignoring everything, stiffly repressing body and mind so that they are like earth or wood—that will never do any good.

When you want to step back, if there are any sayings you do not understand, or any stories you do not comprehend, they are then right before you. Step back and see for yourself why you do not understand.

Doubt and Understanding

If you want to understand Zen, you must question inwardly to study it deeply. If you question deeply, transcendental knowledge appears.

Just You

An ancient Zen master, seeing a monk go down a staircase, called to him, "Reverend!" The monk turned around, whereat the Zen master said, "From birth to old age, it's just you—why turn your head and revolve your brains?"

The monk understood Zen at this remark.

What is this principle? "From birth to old age, it's just you." Tell me, who is this? As soon as you arouse the intention of seeing who you are, you don't see yourself. It is hard to see yourself—very difficult.

People today say, "I am myself—who else?" Ninety-nine out of a hundred understand in this way. What kind of grasp is this on the matter? If you understand in this way, how do you understand the matter of "from birth to old age"? How can you see it's just you?

Personalistic Zen

People these days are just the same as they have been all along, and their capabilities are the same as they have been all along: continuously fluctuating. The reason they are uncertain is because they make up intellectual understandings of the words of ancient Zen teachers, using personalistic approaches.

Misunderstanding

Ancient Zen teachers were so compassionate that they said, "Activity is Buddha activity, sitting is Buddha sitting, all things are Buddha teachings, all sounds are Buddha voices." It is, however, a misunderstanding to think this means all sounds are actually the voice of enlightenment, or that all forms are actually forms of enlightenment.

Fixation

The minute you fixate on the recognition that "This is 'it,' " you are immediately bound hand and foot and cannot move around anymore.

So as soon as it is given this recognition, nothing is right, whatever it may be. If you don't fixate on recognition, you can still be saved.

It's like making a boat and outfitting it for a thousand mile journey to a treasure trove; if you drive a stake and tie the boat to it before you jump in and start rowing, you can row till kingdom come and still be on the beach. You see the boat waving this way and that, and you think you are on the move, but you've never gone a single step.

Know Yourself

I tell people to get to know themselves. Some people think this means what beginners observe, and consider it easy to understand. Reflect more carefully, in a more leisurely manner—what do you call your self?

Misapplication

Buddhism is an easily understood teaching that saves energy, but people cause themselves pains. The ancients saw people helpless, and told them to try meditating quietly. This was good advice, but later people didn't understand what the ancients meant, and closed their eyes, suppressed body and mind, and sat like lumps waiting for enlightenment. How foolish!

Subjective Objects

Objects are defined subjectively. Since objects are defined arbitrarily, this gives rise to your arbitrary subjectivity.

Nonsubjectivity

When you see, let there be no seer or seen; when you hear, let there be no hearer or heard; when you think, let there be no thinker or thought.

Buddhism is extremely easy and saves the most energy. It's just that you yourself waste energy and cause yourself trouble.

The Veil of Light

Some senior Zen students say they don't rationalize at all, don't calculate and compare at all, don't cling to sound and form, don't rest on defilement and purity. They say the sacred and the profane, delusion and enlightenment, are a single clear emptiness. They say there are no such things in the midst of great light. They are veiled by the light of wisdom, fixated on wisdom. They are incurable.

Distorted by a Teacher

The second ancestor of Zen used to give talks wherever he happened to be, and all who heard him attained true awareness. He didn't establish any slogans or talk about causes and effects of practice and realization.

In his time there was a certain meditation teacher who sent a top disciple to listen in on the Zen ancestor. The disciple never came back. The meditation teacher was furious, and took the occasion of a congress to upbraid his former disciple for disloyalty.

The former disciple said, "My perception was originally true, but it was distorted by a teacher."

Later someone asked a Zen master, "Where is my power of perception?" The Zen master said, "It is not obtained from a teacher."

This is the way to attain Zen. An ancient said, "The Way is always with people, but people themselves chase after things."

Turning Things Around

In the scriptures it says, "If you can turn things around, this is the same as enlightenment." How can things be turned around?

Scripture also says, "All appearances are illusory. If you see appearances are not the same as true characteristics, you see where enlightenment comes from."

An ancient Zen master said, "If you deny appearances as you see them, you do not see where enlightenment comes from."

Just step back, stop mental machinations, and try to become aware of all the implications of these sayings. If you suddenly see through, how can you be affected by anything?

What Deludes You?

Only when you actually get to the state where there is neither delusion nor enlightenment are you finally comfortable and conserving the most energy.

But for this you have to be someone who has neither delusion nor enlightenment.

During the twenty-four hours of the day, what is there deluding you? You should make a truthful assessment of yourself.

Where You Cannot Fool Yourself

When you sit meditating and enter into absorption, you should have no concerns or problems in yourself. Try to think independently, all by yourself. Other people don't know what you're doing all the time. You reflect on yourself and see whether what you are doing accords with truth or not. Here you cannot fool yourself.

A Method of Sudden Enlightenment

Just don't arouse the mind or stir thoughts twenty-four hours a day. Then you will understand comprehensive realization all at once.

Seek without Seeking

If you seek, how is that different from pursuing sound and form? If you don't seek, how are you different from earth, wood, or stone? You must seek without seeking.

Misperception

Suppose a bit of filth gets stuck to a man's nose while he is sleeping. When he awakens, unaware of what has happened, he may notice an odor and start smelling his shirt. Thinking his shirt stinks, he takes it off. But then whatever he picks up smells bad to him. He doesn't realize the smell is on his nose.

Someone tells him, but he doesn't believe it. Told to wipe his nose, he refuses.

He'll realize sooner if he wipes off his nose, but when he eventually washes his face he'll find there is no odor. Then he'll find, when he smells things, that they do not stink after all.

Zen study is like this. Those who will not stop and look into themselves go on looking for intellectual understanding. That pursuit of intellectual understanding, seeking rationalizations and making comparisons, is all wrong.

If people would turn their attention back to the self, they would understand everything.

Rationalizations

At other places they either put you to work or sit you still. Here I neither put you to work nor sit you still. This is easy to understand, with a minimum of effort, so why don't you understand? Simply because of your countless clever rationalizations. This is what makes it hard for you to understand.

Ordinary Perceptions and Enlightenment

How can you equate ordinary perceptions with actual sudden enlightenment?

Sudden enlightenment is like when a farmer plowing the fields finds one of the pills of immortality and goes to heaven with his whole family after taking it.

It is also like an ordinary person being made a prime minister.

In Buddhist teachings it says that ordinary perceptions are like a clay pot that has not been fired and therefore cannot be used. You have to bake it in a fire before you can use it. That is like attaining sudden enlightenment.

Zen and Enlightenment

I once asked my teacher, "Is there effective enlightenment in Zen?"

He replied, "How could it be attained without enlightenment? But seek without haste or excitement."

What's Wrong?

For your part, obviously something is wrong with you—that's why you go to others for certainty. If you were all right, why would you go ask others?

What's Right?

I just point out where you're right. If you're wrong, I'll never say you're right. I'll wait until you *are* right. I'll only agree with you when you're right.

I can see everything. When I see people come to me, I know whether they have enlightenment or not, and whether they have understanding or not, like a physician who recognizes an ailment at first sight and knows its nature and whether or not it can be cured.

Someone who has to ask about each symptom to find out what's wrong is a mediocre doctor.

A Doze of Zen

Nowadays there are people who just sit there as they are. At first they are alert, but after a while they get sleepy. Nine out of ten sit there dozing. If you don't know how to work, how can you sit there stubbornly expecting to understand?

Sleeping and Eating Zen

My teacher said, "When you are asleep, study Zen as you sleep. When you are eating, study Zen as you eat."

True, Imitation, and Remnant Zen

Usually it is said that there is true Buddhism, and then there are imitations and remnants. I say that Buddhism does not have true, imitation, and remnant versions. Buddhism is always in the world: if you get the point, it is true; if you miss the point, it is an imitation or a remnant.

Boundaries and Traps

You shouldn't set up limits in boundless openness, but if you set up limitlessness as boundless openness, you've trapped yourself.

This is why those who understand emptiness have no mental image of emptiness.

If people use words to label and describe the mind, they never apprehend the mind, but if they don't use words to label and describe the mind, they still don't apprehend the mind.

Transcending Subject and Object

Those who realize Zen enlightenment transcend subject and object. There is no other mysterious principle besides this.

In the course of ordinary daily activities, when you see colors it is a time of realization, and when you hear sounds it is a time of realization. When you eat and drink, this too is a time of realization. This means all these are times of realization when you transcend subject and object in everything.

This is not a matter of long practice, and doesn't need cultivation. It is right here, yet worldly people don't recognize it.

So it is said, "Only with experiential realization do you know the unfathomable."

Natural Revelation

The Way is not only evident after explanation and demonstration, because it is always being revealed naturally.

Explanation and demonstration are expedients used to enable you to realize intuitive understanding; they are only temporary hyways.

Whether you attain realization through explanation, or enter in through demonstration, or reach the goal by spontaneous sensing through individual awareness, ultimately there is no different thing or separate attainment.

It is just a matter of reaching the source of mind.

A Sacred Cow

People studying Zen today think dialogue is essential to the Zen school. They do not realize this is grasping and rejecting, producing imagination.

Check Yourself

You must know how to check yourself before you can attain Zen. It is because of confused minds that people strive on the Way; they go to mountains and forests to see teachers, on the false assumption that there is a particular path that can give people peace and comfort. They do not know it is best to work on finding out where they got confused.

Oversimplified Zen

Many people today consider the immediate mirrorlike awareness to be the ultimate rule. This is why an ancient master said, "Does it exist where there are no people?"

The Power of the Way

For those who arrive on the Way, everything is "it." This power is very great.

It is only the infection of endless false consciousness that makes the function of the power defective.

ZEN MASTER DAHUI

The Realm of the Enlightened

The Flower Ornament Scripture says, "If you want to know the realm of the enlightened, you should make your mind as clear as space; detach from subjective imaginings and from all grasping, making your mind unimpeded wherever it turns."

The realm of the enlightened is not an external realm with manifest characteristics; buddhahood is the realm of the sacred knowledge found in oneself.

You do not need paraphernalia, practices, or realizations to attain it—what you need to do is to clean out the influences of the psychological afflictions connected with the external world that have been accumulating in your psyche since beginningless time.

Make your mind as wide open as cosmic space; detach from graspings in the conceptual consciousness, and false ideas and imaginings will also be like empty space. Then this effortless subtle mind will naturally be unimpeded wherever it turns.

See Buddha Everywhere

The Flower Ornament Scripture says, "Do not see Buddha in one phenomenon, one event, one body, one land, one being—see Buddha everywhere."

Buddha means awake, being aware everywhere and always. Seeing Buddha everywhere means seeing your own inherent natural Buddha in the fundamental wellspring of your self.

There is not a single time, a single place, a single phenomenon, a single event, a single body, a single land, a single realm of being, where this is not present.

Discontinuing Thoughts

When you are studying Zen, as you meet with people and deal with situations, never let bad thoughts continue. If you come up with a bad thought unawares, immediately focus your attention and root the thought out. If you just follow that thought and continue such thinking uninterrupted, this will not only hinder Zen realization, it will make you a fool.

Mind Your Own Business

"Don't draw another's bow, don't ride another's horse, don't mind another's business."

Although this is a common saying, it can also help you penetrate Zen.

Just examine yourself constantly—from morning to night, what have you done that is beneficial to others and to yourself?

If you notice any partiality, you should alert yourself and not overlook it.

No Mind

"When you have no mind, Zen is easy to find."

In Zen terminology, "mindlessness" does not mean insensitivity or ignorance. It means that the mind is stable and does not get stirred up by the situations and circumstances one encounters; it means the mind does not grasp anything, it is clear in all situations, unimpeded and undefiled, not dwelling on anything, even nondefilement.

The Purpose of Stillness

Those who study Zen should be mentally quiet twenty-four hours a day. When you have nothing to do, you should also sit quietly, making the mind alert and the body tranquil.

Eventually, when you are thoroughly practiced in this, body and mind become spontaneously peaceful and calm, and you have some direction in Zen.

The perfection of mental silence is only to settle scattered and confused awareness. If you cling to stillness as ultimate, you will be taken in by the false Zen of silent illumination.

The Source of Mind

Good and bad come from your own mind. But what do you call your own mind, apart from your actions and thoughts? Where does your own mind come from?

If you really know where your own mind comes from, boundless obstacles caused by your own actions will be cleared all at once.

After that, all sorts of extraordinary possibilities will come to you without your seeking them.

The Natural State

If you want to empty all things, first clean your own mind. When your mind is clear and clean, all entanglements cease.

Once entanglements cease, both substance and function are in their natural state. "Substance" means the clear, pure, original source of your own mind; the "function" is your own mind's marvelous function of change and creation, which enters into both purity and defilement without being affected by or attached to either purity or defilement.

Adaptation

In ancient times, Zen teaching was sometimes abstract, sometimes concrete, sometimes based on a particular time, sometimes transcendental. There was no fixed standard at all.

Real Zen

If you think there are any verbal formulations that are special mysterious secrets to be transmitted, this is not real Zen.

Real Zen has no transmission. It is just a matter of people experiencing it, resulting in their ability to see each other's vision and communicate tacitly.

Your Own Business

Zen is not in quietude, nor is it in clamor. It is not in thought and discrimination, nor is it in dealing with daily affairs. But even so, it is most important that you not abandon quiet and clamor, dealing with daily affairs, or thought and discrimination, in order to study Zen. When your eyes open, you will find all these are your own business.

Foul Weather Zen

Many people who study Zen are in a burning rush to learn Zen when their worldly affairs are not to their satisfaction, but then give up Zen when they become successful in the world.

Peace and Quiet

When you have attained mental and physical peace and quiet, don't get stuck in peace and quiet. Be independent and free, like a gourd rolling and bobbing on a river.

Living Zen

To attain Zen enlightenment, it is not necessary to give up family life, quit your job, become a vegetarian, practice asceticism, and flee to a quiet place, then go into a ghost cave of dead Zen to entertain subjective imaginings.

Degenerate Zennism

In modern times, Zen and Buddhism have become extremely degenerate. There are incompetent teachers who basically lack enlightenment themselves and have chaotic, unreliable consciousness. Lacking true skills, they take in students and teach everyone to be like themselves.

Quiet Meditation

If you have been practicing quiet meditation but your mind is still not calm and free when in the midst of activity, this means you haven't been empowered by your quiet meditation.

If you have been practicing quietude just to get rid of agitation, then when you are in the midst of agitation, the agitation will disturb your mind just as if you had never done any quiet meditation.

Saving Energy

People are backwards—ignorant of the true self, they pursue things, willingly suffering immeasurable pains in their greed for a little bit of pleasure. In the mornings, before they've opened their eyes and gotten out of bed, when they're still only half awake, their minds are already flying about in confusion, flowing along with random thoughts. Although good and bad deeds have not yet appeared, heaven and hell are already formed in their hearts before they even get out of bed. By the time they go into action, the seeds of heaven and hell are already implanted in their minds.

Did not the Buddha say, "All faculties of sense are receptacles manifested by your own mind. Physical bodies are manifestations of your own minds' representations of forms as subjectively imagined. These manifestations are like the flow of a river, like seeds, like a lamp, like wind, passing away from instant to instant. Frenetic activity, attraction to impure things, and voracity are the causes of the useless, deceptive habits that seem to have always existed, like a waterwheel always turning."

If you really see through this, you understand the meaning of impersonality. You know that heaven and hell are nowhere else but in the heart of the half awake individual about to get out of bed—they do not come from outside.

While in the process of waking up, you should really pay

attention. While you are paying attention, you should not make any effort to struggle with whatever is going on in your mind. While struggling you waste energy. As the third ancestor of Zen said, "If you try to stop movement and return to stillness, the attempt to be still will increase movement."

When you notice that you are saving energy in the midst of the mundane stress of daily affairs, this is where you gain energy, this is where you attain buddhahood, this is where you turn hell into heaven.

Zen Hobbyists

There are intellectual professionals who think they know everything but Zen, so they call over a few incompetent old monks, give them a meal, and have them say whatever comes into their minds. The intellectuals then write this babble down and use it to judge everyone else. They trade sayings and call this Zen encounter, imagining they have gotten the advantage if they get in the last word.

They don't even know it if they happen to run into real perceptives. Even if they do notice the real ones, these intellectuals are not really sure, and will not sincerely seek understanding from the teachers. They just seek approval as before. Then when the teachers demonstrate the real developmental impact of Zen in the midst of all sorts of situations, the intellectuals are afraid to approach.

Looking for the Shortcut

When you have even a single thought of looking for a shortcut in Zen, you have already stuck your head in a bowl of glue.

Attunement

Many people today study Zen acquisitively—this is truly a false idea about what has no false ideas.

Just make your mind free. But don't be too tense, and don't be too loose—working this way will save you unlimited mental energy.

Liberation

People have been used by the mind's conceptual consciousness since before they can remember, flowing in the waves of birth and death, unable to be independent. If they want to leave birth and death to be joyfully alive, they must cut through decisively, stopping the course of mind's conceptual consciousness.

Zen Sects

In Zen, there are no sectarian differences, but when students lack a broad, stable will, and teachers lack a broad, comprehensive teaching, then what they enter into differs. The ultimate point of Zen, however, has no such differences.

Past, Present, and Future

Buddha said that when the mind does not grasp things of the past, does not long for things of the future, and does not dwell on things of the present, then one realizes that past, present, and future are empty.

Don't think about past events, whether good or bad, for if you think about them, this impedes the Way. Don't calculate future matters, for if you calculate, you go mad. Don't fix your attention on present affairs, whether unpleasant or pleasant, for if you fix your attention on them, they will disturb your mind.

Just deal with situations as they happen, and you will spontaneously accord with these principles.

ZEN MASTER HONGZHI

The Subtlety of Zen

To learn the subtlety of Zen, you must clarify your mind and immerse your spirit in silent exercise of inner gazing. When you see into the source of reality, with no obstruction whatsoever, it is open and formless, like water in autumn, clear and bright, like the moon taking away the darkness of night.

Finding Out for Oneself

The mind originally is detached from objects, reality basically has no explanation. This is why a classical Zen master said, "Our school has no slogans, and no doctrine to give people." Fundamentally it is a matter of people arriving on their own and finding out for themselves; only then can they talk about it.

Zen Mind

Just wash away the dust and dirt of subjective thoughts immediately. When the dust and dirt are washed away, your mind is open, shining brightly, without boundaries, without center or extremes. Completely whole, radiant with light, it shines through the universe, cutting through past, present, and future.

This is inherent in you, and does not come from outside. This is called the state of true reality. One who has experienced this can enter into all sorts of situations in response to all sorts of possibilities, with subtle function that is marvelously effective and naturally uninhibited.

Everyone's Zen

Ever since the time of the Buddha and the founders of Zen, there has never been any distinction between ordained and lay people, in the sense that everyone who has accurate personal experience of true realization is said to have entered the school of the enlightened mind and penetrated the source of religion.

Zen Experience

When you are empty and spontaneously aware, clean and spontaneously clear, you are capable of panoramic consciousness without making an effort to grasp perception, and you are capable of discerning understanding without the burden of conditioned thought. You go beyond being and nothingness, and transcend conceivable feelings. This is only experienced by union with it—it is not gotten from another.

Zen Life, Zen Action

The wordly life of people who have mastered Zen is buoyant and unbridled, like clouds making rain, like the moon in a stream, like an orchid in a recondite spot, like spring in living beings. Their action is not self-conscious, yet their responses have order. This is what those who have mastered Zen do.

It is also necessary to turn back to the source, to set foot on the realm of peace, plunge into the realm of purity, and stand alone, without companions, going all the way through the road beyond the buddhas. Only then can you fully comprehend the center and the extremes, penetrate the very top and the very bottom, and freely kill and enliven, roll up and roll out.

Autumn and Spring

When Zen practice is completely developed, there is no center, no extremes; there are no edges or corners. It is perfectly round and frictionless.

It is also necessary to be empty, open, and unpolluted, so "the clear autumn moon cold, its shining light washes the night. Brocade clouds flower prettily, the atmosphere turns into spring."

The Light of Mind

When material sense doesn't blind you, all things are seen to be the light of mind. You transcend with every step, on the path of the bird, no tarrying anywhere. You respond to the world with clarity, open awareness unstrained.

Spontaneous Knowledge

All realms of phenomena arise from one mind. When the one mind is quiescent, all appearances end. Then which is other, which is self?

Because there are no differentiated appearances at such a time, nothing at all is defined, not a single thought is produced—you pass beyond before birth and after death; the mind becomes a point of subtle light, round and frictionless, without location, without traces. Then your mind cannot be obscured.

This point where there can be no obscuration is called spontaneous knowledge. Just this realm of spontaneous knowledge is called the original attainment. Nothing whatsoever is attained from outside.

Zen Mastery

The action and repose of those who have mastered Zen are like flowing clouds, without self-consciousness, like the full moon, reflected everywhere. People who have mastered Zen are not stopped by anything: though clearly in the midst of all things, still they are highly aloof; though they encounter experiences according to circumstances, they are not tainted or mixed up by them.

Aloof of the Tumult

When you understand and arrive at the emptiness of all things, then you are independent of every state of mind, and transcend every situation. The original light is everywhere, and you then adapt to the potential at hand; everything you meet is Zen.

While subtly aware of all circumstances, you are empty and have no subjective stance towards them. Like the breeze in the pines, the moon in the water, there is a clear and light harmony. You have no coming and going mind, and you do not linger over appearances.

The essence is in being inwardly open and accommodating while outwardly responsive without unrest. Be like spring causing the flowers to bloom, like a mirror reflecting images, and you will naturally emerge aloof of all tumult.

Normalcy

The time when you "see the sun in daytime and see the moon at night," when you are not deceived, is the normal behavior of a Zen practitioner, naturally without edges or seams. If you want to attain this kind of normalcy, you have to put an end to the subtle pounding and weaving that goes on in your mind.

Enlightened Awareness

Buddhas and Zen masters do not have different realizations; they all reach the point of cessation, where past, present, and future are cut off and all impulses stop, where there is not the slightest object. Enlightened awareness shines spontaneously, subtly penetrating the root source.

Shedding Your Skin

The experience described as shedding your skin, transcending reflections of subjective awareness, where no mental machinations can reach, is not transmitted by sages. It can only be attained inwardly, by profound experience of spontaneous illumination. The original light destroys the darkness, real illumination mirrors the infinite. Subjective assessments of what is or is not are all transcended.

ZEN MASTER YING-AN

Zen Mind

The mind of Zen adepts is straight as a bowstring, like a long sword against the sky cutting through confusion wherever they may be. Wordly wealth and status, hauteur and extravagance, mundane desires, and all the ups and downs of life, cannot affect them. Fame and profit, judgments of right and wrong, and all the possible states of being, cannot trap them.

Freedom

When you pass through, no one can pin you down, no one can call you back.

Destroying Zen

Some people gain an insight and then sit fast on this insight, so their perception is not free. They talk about mystery and marvel, setting forth byways and thinking they are thus helping people. They are destroying Zen.

There is another type of person who cultivates a state of quietude, so their bodies and minds feel somewhat light and calm, and then sit fanatically in the realm where there are no people. When they see others telling of good things, they get irritated and upset, and counter that there is basically nothing in the way of Zen to explain.

This is what an ancient master called a sickness characterized by lack of clarity in all places, in which there appears to be something present. This malady is most miserable.

There are those who get this point of view and then deny everything—there are no buddhas, no Zen masters, no sages. They go on denying, doing whatever they want and calling that "unobstructed Zen."

This is what another ancient master called "Having a vast realization of emptiness, then trying to deny the effects of causes, becoming wild and unrestrained, bringing on disaster."

There is also a type whose point of view is oblivious silence, not hearing anything. After they have eaten of the community's food, they just sit there as if dead, waiting for enlightenment.

People like this are clumps of clay in ramshackle huts in the deep mountains and broad wastelands. They might think they are Buddhist masters with unchanging wisdom, but they are just using up the alms of the faithful.

Real Zen students never have any such resorts; they have in themselves a life transcending religious or sectarian "Zen," with independent perception.

The First Step

The beginning of cultivating yourself is right in yourself; on a thousand mile journey, the first step is the most important. If you can do both of these well, the infinite sublime meanings of hundreds of thousands of teachings will be fulfilled.

The Subtlety of Zen

In Zen, your eyes are looking southeast while your attention is in the northwest. It cannot be sought by mindlessness, it cannot be understood by mindfulness. It cannot be reached by talking, it cannot be understood by silence.

Nothing to Grab

Zen has nothing to grab onto. When people who study Zen don't see it, that is because they approach too eagerly.

65

If you want to understand Zen easily, just be mindless, wherever you are, twenty-four hours a day, until you spontaneously merge with the Way.

Once you merge with the Way, inside, outside, or in-between cannot be found at all—you experience a frozen emptiness, totally independent.

This is what an ancient worthy called "The mind not touching things, the steps not placed anywhere."

Original Zen

Early on, Zen was mastered and borne by exceptional people, because unperceptive and impulsive people cannot work it or hold it. All the original adepts were unique in their speech and activity, never willing to sink into stagnancy, as if there were a final form of Zen.

Zen Understanding

First of all, don't establish a preconceived understanding of Zen, yet don't rationalize Zen as "not understanding" either.

It's just like learning archery: eventually you reach a point where ideas are ended and feelings forgotten, and then you suddenly hit the target.

You should also know, furthermore, that there is a subtlety breaking through the target, which is attained spontaneously.

Zen Practice

Zen cannot be attained by lectures, discussions, and debates. Only those of great perceptive capacity can clearly understand it.

For this reason the ancient adepts did not waste a moment. Even when they weren't calling on teachers to ascertain specific truths, they were involved in real Zen practice, so they eventually attained mature serenity in a natural way. They were not wrapped up in the illusions of the world.

If you can do this, at some point you will suddenly turn the light of your mind around and see through illusions to the real self. Then you will understand where everything comes from—mundane passions and illusions, the material world, form and emptiness, light and darkness, principle and essence, mystery and marvel.

Once you understand this clearly, then you will not be caged or trapped by anything at all, mundane or transmundane.

False Zen, True Zen

There are two kinds of Zen students who won't let go. One kind consists of those who did not meet real teachers at the outset of their quest, plunged into the fires of false teachers, and having been poisoned by their venom, they think their Zen study is done.

Another kind consists of those who join Zen groups and call themselves Zen students but really lack the correct basis. They just usurp what they hear, eager to be known for it, trying to prove themselves, only saying that Zen is just this.

These two kinds of people are fatally ill, unless they recognize their error someday and let go of it sometime.

But what are people in these conditions to let go of, after all? Just let go of the burden of "others" and "self," of ideas of gain and loss, right and wrong, Buddha and Buddhism, mystery and marvel.

As soon as you let go this way, you feel body and mind light and easy, thoroughly pure inside and out. Then your heart is clear all the time. In a cool flash of insight, you go free.

Now you are ready for refinement. If you just keep to the insight you've attained and consider it ultimate, you are still clinging to something. Zen people free from convention are very different from this.

Chills and Fever

If mature people want to cut off the road of birth and death, they should relinquish what they have been holding dear, so that their senses become clean and naked. One day they will gain insight, and the road of birth and death is sure to end.

If you don't practice this in reality, but desire a lot of intellectual knowledge, thinking this is the wonder of self-realization, your chills and fever will be increased by the wind of intellectual knowledge; your nose will always be stuffy and your head will always be foggy.

Lone Lamp Zen

If people want to learn Zen, let them learn the Zen of a lone lamp shining in a death ward.

Do not set up any limit, with the idea that you want to realize Zen for sure by such and such a time.

Imitation Zen

There are people who go wrong because they do not comprehend Zen methodology. Some think stonewalling is great, some think utter silence is the ultimate rule, some think literary activity is versatility.

Zen Living

Zen living is a most direct shortcut, not requiring the exertion of the slightest bit of strength to attain enlightenment and master Zen right where you are.

But because Zen seekers are searching too eagerly, they think there must be a special principle, so they try to describe it to themselves mentally, in a subjective way.

Thus they are swept by the machinations of emotive and intellectual consciousness into something that is created and will perish.

They cling to this created, perishable law, rule, principle, or way of life, as something ultimate. This is a serious misstep.

This is why it is said, "Do not talk about ultimate reality with your mind on what is created and destructible."

Personalistic Zen

Many Zennists cling to personalistic views as ultimate realities or final truths, and do not believe there can be anything better. As soon as they are put to a real Zen test, they are lost.

This happens when they finally never meet a real Zen master, so their realization is crude. They sit in a nest of "win or lose," fearing to be disturbed by anyone, afraid they'll lose Zen.

Some Zennists say their viewpoints are all correct, and when experienced masters tell them it is not so, they say this is just a deliberate ploy to entrap them and pull them around.

These paranoid Zennists stop after they have merely managed to hold still. This is a fatal disease, which is of its own nature incurable. Therefore all Zen seekers can do is to be careful to avoid it.

The Zen of Essence

When the essence of seeing is everywhere, so is the essence of hearing. When you clearly penetrate the ten directions, there is no inside or outside. This is why it is said, "Effortless in all circumstances, always real in action and stillness." Action like this is the function of complete real wisdom.

Greatness

The ancient Zen masters did not have a single thought of trying to become great people. Only thus did they attain mastery of life and death, and after that greatness came of itself.

If you have a single thought of eagerness to attain Zen mastery, this burns out your potential, so you cannot grow anymore.

Looking for Approval

Nowadays when Zennists see respected masters, they don't ask what to do—all they want is to be told they have some insight. It delights them to hear themselves recognized, unaware that by indulging in this delight they are asking for trouble.

Ancient Zen Practice

The classical masters of Zen were people who had above all let go.

69

As soon as they showed up, they overturned the sky and wrapped up the earth.

How was it that they were like this?

Simply because their final thought was correct and they couldn't be trapped by false teachers or mountebanks and mesmerists, so their mentalities were beyond clannishness and transcended conventional parameters.

They did not associate with people at random, and they did not dwell on anything ephemeral.

They only kept life and death uppermost in their minds, and yet as they did so they did not suppose there is anything that dies or does not die.

This is how the ancients worked. In this it is essential to penetrate clearly and extend it to full application.

After that, one can undergo radical Zen treatment, lest one still be at a loss in the midst of complex changes and developments.

Needless to say, when one is still at a stage where the mind is "half dark and half light, half clear and half raining," one cannot "walk alone in the vastness" even if one wants to.

Graduate Zen

"Enlightenment is beyond words, and no person has ever attained it."

A classical Zen master said, "Zen has no sayings, nothing at all to give people."

Another classical master said, "I don't like to hear the word 'Buddha.'"

See how they sprayed sand and hurled stones this way. This can already blind people. If you still look for a living road on a staff or search for a representative expression in a shout, this is no different from catching a rat and looking in its mouth for elephant tusks.

This is why the classical Zen masters preserved a certain state, in which no time whatsoever is wasted twenty-four hours a day.

This state is to be maintained until you reach the point where there is nowhere to grasp and nowhere to anchor.

Then you should let go and make yourself empty and quiet, clear and calm, to the point where former intellectual interpretation, rationalization, misknowledge, and misperception, cannot get into your mind or act on it at all.

This is the essential shortcut to the Way. Do this, and one day you will clearly understand what's going on where you are.

Empowering Will

Generally speaking, Zen requires a decisive, powerful will, because you are going to be cleaning your six senses all the time, so that even if you are in the midst of all the stresses and pleasures of the world, it is like being in a pure, uncontrived realm of great liberation.

Profoundly stable and calm, like a gigantic mountain, you cannot be disturbed by cravings or external conditions, you cannot be held back by interference and difficulty.

This is a shortcut to the Way by empowered work.

The Subtle Mind of Zen

If you want to see the subtle mind of Zen, that is very easy. Just step back and pick it up with intense strength during all of your activities, whatever you are doing, even as you eat, drink, and talk, even as you experience the stress of attending to the world.

ZEN MASTER MI-AN

The Living Road

*A*ll people have their own living road to heaven. Until they walk on this road, they are like drunkards who cannot tell which way is which.

Then when they set foot on this road and lose their confusion, it is up to them which way they shall go—they are no longer subject to the arbitrary directions of others.

Totally Alive

When you are totally alive and cannot be trapped or caged, only then do you have some independence. Then you can be in the ordinary world all day long without it affecting you.

Deluded Zen

Many people study Zen, but encounter Zen teachers without clear perception of truth. They make arbitrary explanations and take their subjective interpretations of Zen sayings for final truths. Their aim is to be recognized as understanding Zen. This is a most serious malady.

Zen Malfunctions

When people study Zen diligently but do not attain enlightenment, their problem may be in a number of places.

It may be in getting bogged down in Zen sayings.

It may be in sitting transfixed in a realm of surpassing wonder.

It may be in empty formlessness.

It may be in keeping Zen or Buddhism on one's mind.

It may be in trying to reject illusion for enlightenment.

It may be in not having met a real enlightened teacher at the outset and thus having been drawn into a nest of complications.

These problems are not experienced only by beginners. Even ancient Zen masters who had thoroughly understood the basic mind and seen into its fundamental nature realized the original state but still did not understand the whole truth.

The Zen Shortcut

The shortcut of Zen is to leave the present and directly experience the state before birth, before the division of wholeness.

When you accomplish this, you are like a dragon in the water, like a tiger in the mountains. You are very clear and calm everywhere, free to enliven or kill everywhere, spontaneously able to "rouse the wind and stir the grasses" everywhere. You do not cling to any activity, you do not sit inactive.

This is like cutting a skein of thread, and dyeing a skein of thread—when one is cut all are cut, when one is dyed all are dyed. From top to bottom, the whole thing is a huge door of liberation. Now Buddhist truths and things of the world have become one—where is there any external thing at all to constitute an impediment?

ZEN MASTER XIATANG

The Perception of Sages

The Scripture on Infinite Light says, "Rivers, lakes, birds, trees, and forests all invoke Buddha, Truth, and Communion."

In a moment of awareness without discrimination, great wisdom appears. This is like pouring water into the ocean, like working a bellows in the wind.

Furthermore, how do you discriminate? 'Buddha' is a temporary name for what cannot be seen when you look, what cannot be heard when you listen, whose place of origin and passing away cannot be found when you search.

It covers form and sound, pervades sky and earth, penetrates above and below. There is no second view, no second person, no second thought. It is everywhere, in everything, not something external.

This is why the single source of all awareness is called 'Buddha.'

It doesn't change when the body deteriorates, it is always there. But you still cannot use what is always there. Why? Because, as the saying goes, "Although gold dust is precious, when it gets in your eyes it obstructs vision." Although buddhahood is wonderful, if you are obsessed with it it becomes a sickness.

An early Zen master said, "It is not mind, not Buddha, not a thing—what is it?" This says it all. It has brought us the diamond sword that cuts through all obsessions.

Another classical Zen master said, "The slightest entangling thought can cause hellish actions; a flash of feeling can chain you indefinitely. Just end ordinary feelings, and there is no special perception of sages to seek—the perception of sages appears where ordinary feelings end."

Breaking Habits

To learn to be a Buddha, first you should break through the seeds of habit with great determination, and then be aware of cause and effect so that you fear to do wrong. Transcend all mental objects, stop all rumination. Don't let either good or bad thoughts enter into your thinking, forget about both Buddhism and things of the world. Let go of body and mind, like letting go over a cliff. Be like space, not producing subjective thoughts of life and death, or any signs of discrimination. If you have any views at all, cut them right off and don't let them continue.

ZEN MASTER YUANSOU

The Crowning Meditation

*I*f you do not listen truly, you will call the bell a pitcher, and inevitably wind up adding error to error, talking about "Buddha," "Zen masters," "mind," and "essence." How is this different from gouging a wound in healthy flesh?

Real Zennists set a single eye on the state before the embryo is formed, before any signs become distinct. This opens up and clears the mind, so that it penetrates the whole universe. Then they are no different from the Buddha and the founder of Zen.

This is called the crowning meditation, the jewel that reflects all colors, the inexhaustible treasury, the gateway to spiritual powers, the diamond sword, the crouching lion, the blaze—there are various names for it.

Now there is nothing in the universe, nothing mundane or transmundane, to be an object, an opposite, a barrier, or a hindrance to you.

Expedients and Reality

The mountains, rivers, earth, grasses, trees, and forests, are always emanating a subtle, precious light, day and night, always emanating a subtle, precious sound, demonstrating and expounding to all people the unsurpassed ultimate truth.

It is just because you miss it right where you are, or avoid it even as you face it, that you are unable to attain actual use of it.

This is why Buddhism came into being, with its many expedients and clever explanations, with temporary and true, immediate and gradual, half and full, partial and complete teachings. These are all simply means of stopping children from whining.

It

Those who meditate in silent stillness regard silent stillness as final, but it is not something to finalize in stillness. Those who assert mastery in the midst of busyness are satisfied with busyness, but it is not something to be satisfied with in the midst of busyness. Those who learn from the scriptures consider the scriptures basic, but it is not learned from the scriptures. Those who work with teachers and colleagues regard this as a profound source, but it is not attained from working with teachers and colleagues.

It is a formless, indestructible being that has always been like a fish hidden in a spring, that drums up waves and dances by itself. When you look for it in the east, it goes west; when you look for it in the south, it goes north. It can give names to everyone, but no one can give it a name. In all places and all times it is the master of myriad forms, the teacher of myriad phenomena.

Distortion by Teachers

The "one road beyond" is vast as cosmic space times ten; it cannot be sought with mind, it cannot be attained by mindlessness. It cannot be reached by words, it cannot be understood by silence. The essential point is for the individual to be firm in faith and see right through the state before the embryo is formed, before any signs become distinct.

Passing through the heights and the depths, escaping all traps, ranging over all time, totally without attachment and repulsion, free in all ways, when you attain great independence you have some measure of accord with the one road beyond.

If you rely on the differences in teachers and see the differences in persons, you are misled by blind teachers into reifying Buddha, Dharma, Zen, Tao, mysteries, marvels, functions, and states. One way and another this glues your tongue down, nails your eyes shut, and constricts your heart.

Like oil getting into flour, this becomes deeply ingrained, until you eventually become a sprite or a ghoul, emanating countless "lights" and manifesting countless "psychic powers," thinking you are peerless in all the world. This is what is meant by the saying, "Our perception is originally correct, but it is distorted by teachers."

Liberation

This inconceivable door of great liberation is in everyone. It has never been blocked, it has never been defective. Buddhas and Zen masters have appeared in the world and provided expedient methods, with many different devices, using illusory medicines to cure illusory illnesses, just because your faculties are unequal, your knowledge is unclear, you do not transcend what you see and hear as you see and hear it, and you are tumbled about endlessly in an ocean of misery by afflictions due to ignorance, by emotional views and habitual conceptions of others and self, right and wrong.

The various teachings and techniques of buddhas and Zen masters are only set forth so that you will individually step back into yourself, understand your own original mind and see your own original nature, so that you reach a state of great rest, peace, and happiness.

Bad Habits

In the root and stem of your own psyche there is an accumulation of bad habits. If you cannot see through them and act independently of them, you will unavoidably get bogged down along the way.

Spontaneous Zen

In Buddhism there is no place to apply effort. Everything in it is normal—you put on clothes to keep warm and eat food to stop hunger—that's all. If you consciously try to think about it, it is not what you think of. If you consciously try to arrange it, it is not what you arrange.

Expedients

Buddhist teachings are prescriptions given according to specific ailments, to clear away the roots of your compulsive habits and clean out your emotional views, just so you can be free and clear, naked and clean, without problems.

There is no real doctrine at all for you to chew on or squat over. If you will not believe in yourself, you pick up your baggage and go around to other people's houses looking for Zen, looking for Tao, looking for mysteries, looking for marvels, looking for buddhas, looking for Zen masters, looking for teachers.

You think this is searching for the ultimate, and you make it into your religion, but this is like running blindly to the east to get something that is in the west. The more you run, the further away you are, and the more you hurry the later you become. You just tire yourself, to what benefit in the end?

Zen Mind

The mind of people of the Way is straight as a bowstring. Simply because they are not burdened by ideas of others and themselves, of right and wrong, of sacred and profane, of better and worse, or by deception, falsehood, flattery, or deviousness, they spontaneously gain access to the substance of mind that dwells on nothing.

Fundamentally this is not another, not oneself, not ordinary, not holy, not mind, not Buddha, not a thing, not Zen, not Tao, not a mystery, not a marvel.

It is only because of a moment of subjectivity in discrimination, grasping and rejecting, that so many horns are suddenly produced on your head and you are turned about by those myriad objects all the time, unable to be free and independent.

Reflections on the Science of Freedom

Someone asked one of the early Zen masters to teach him a way to liberation.

The Zen master said, "Who binds you?"
The seeker of liberty said, "No one binds me."
The Zen master said, "Then why seek liberation?"

Liberation of the human mind from the inhibiting effects of mesmerism by its own creations is the essence of Zen. This liberation is seen on the one hand in terms of freeing the mind from uncomfortable and unnecessary limitations and on the other in terms of freeing the "great potential and great function" dormant in the unknown realm of conscious action beyond those limitations. Early Zen masters revived the teaching of Buddha that liberation is the essential criterion of spiritual authenticity, not tradition or convention.

In modern times it has become customary to think of bondage primarily in social, political, or economic terms. Emotional, intellectual, and more subtle forms of bondage are commonly associated with side effects or secondary developments of more obvious forms of oppression, such as those visible in material or institutional terms. Bondage is often seen primarily as something imposed from without, while its internal manifestations are regarded as reactions or adaptations to the external condition.

Buddhist thought, on the other hand, sees mind as the ultimate source of bondage, whether imposed by others or self-imposed. If this is true, it explains why social liberation and reform movements that work on the symptoms of bondage and injustice without effectively addressing their source are never completely or finally effective. History tells of political liberators who became oppressors in turn; of organizations originally set up to protect rights turning into usurpers of rights; of institutions ostensibly established to free people from ignorance becoming little more than tools for the imprisonment of minds within the boundaries of received opinion.

According to Zen teaching, the quest for freedom itself has the power to bind, whether it be acted out in psychological, political, or religious terms. Buddhism insists that real freedom is possible, even if its price includes the very myths and illusions that may have once inspired this aspiration. Just as mind is considered by Buddhists to be the source of bondage, it is also considered to be the source of enlightenment. Buddhists believe that unimaginable capacities for fulfillment lie hidden in the mind, concealed by the preoccupations of day-to-day concerns and worries.

Who binds us? Buddhism says we bind ourselves in the web of our individual and collective ideas, words, and acts. This is held true of everything from personal neuroses to massive oppressions, from self-inflicted suffering to the suffering that people impose on their neighbors. Furthermore, these ideas, words, and acts are observed to emerge from subtle attitudes or mental postures that unconsciously potentiate them and sustain their continuity.

Since these postures are rarely given conscious critical examination, screened as they are by their own subjectivity, the beginning of bondage, from the development of the characteristic inclinations these inner attitudes foster and the reinforcement they attract, is in Zen terminology called "tying yourself up without rope."

From a Zen point of view, the problem underlying diverse manifestations of bondage is a fundamental confusion. In classic Zen terms, this is expressed as mistaking the servant for the master, or taking a guest for the host. Even obvious forms of bondage, such as the political and economic enslavement of peoples, begin and develop into repetitious cycles from the domination of minds by ideas, words, and acts. Buddhist thinking recognizes the susceptibility of the mind to suggestion and conditioning, hence the proverb, "Be master of mind rather than mastered by mind."

While it is understood that nothing can be said about an absolute objectivity totally beyond the mind that supposes it, Buddhism strives for the greatest possible objectivity in understanding humanity, free from the biases and prejudices that blight human relations and prevent humankind from seeing itself as it is. In order to accomplish this, Buddhism examines the relationship between subjectivity and objectivity from every possible angle to arrive at the limits of what can be known about what is real and what is true.

Until one reaches the point where this critical discernment can be made, Zen liberation is not really possible. People may feel liberated when all they have had is a change of concern. They may feel justified when they are only convinced they are right, and these feelings may be all they really want. Then again, people may feel relieved to be having things to do, think about, and talk about, without this really satisfying them or nourishing them inwardly; they may be, in Zen terms, stuffed but not fulfilled. People may feel impelled by conscience to act in ways that do not achieve what they envision because they cannot master the will and knowledge of which their impulses are echoes. All the problems of psychological and spiritual inauthenticity are placed under the rigorous scrutiny of the Zen eye. Zen drives at the reality of freedom, not the image of freedom.

An age-old Zen observation has been that whatever stimulates or motivates people, whether it be expressed in economic, political, social, psychological, or religious terms, may in fact be inhibiting them from fulfilling the very needs and desires that stimulate and motivate them. In Zen terms this does not mean that the object in itself thwarts anyone, but that the individual's conception of the object and attitude toward it are unfulfilling.

Here is the crux of the Zen approach to liberation. The shackles of poverty and oppression are visible to the ordinary eye, and it is not hard to find agreement in sympathy for those thus afflicted. Often, however, people—and peoples—are chained by shackles that they in fact treasure. As one Zen master said, it is hard for people to see anything wrong with what they like, or to see anything good in what they do not like. Another Zen master noted that familiarity itself is a quality that people are generally inclined to like. This means that predilections and habits with which people feel comfortable at a given time may serve them for comfort but may in fact be holding them back from greater capacity for progress and fulfillment.

Like Taoism, its ancient predecessor, Zen has long observed that one of the predilections contrary to real progress in social and individual development is the desire for rapid and visible results. Countless studies have shown that the results of haste in social and political affairs are similar to the results of haste in psychological studies—depression, resentment, regret, and longing, which eventually consume any temporary gains that might have been made. What is finally left of this process, after emotions are exhausted, is a collection of rationalizations, in themselves as ineffective as emotions alone.

It is sometimes asked, for example, why massive hunger and

oppression continue to exist in spite of large quantities of surplus wealth and elaborate systems of law and government. Searching for an answer to this conundrum, a political thinker might focus mainly on the interplay of conflicting material interests involved and the influence of interlopers. A social scientist might advance theories resorting to peculiarities of culture and history to explain the persistence of involutionary social patterns. A Zen observer would, however, have to consider the entire nexus of conditions impartially, without isolating any one element because of emotional associations.

In order to understand truthfully what is really possible in a given situation, the would-be illuminate may have to stand aside from inculcated ideals and sacrifice sentimental compassion. This is part of the "great death" Zen practitioners seek in order to clarify their minds and see what is before them impersonally and impartially, so that they may start life fresh without the burden of past illusions.

One of the most attractive illusions of modern times has been the popular myth that freedom can be gained and safeguarded simply by appropriately designed systems of organization and government. While one system may prove more effective than another under given conditions, nevertheless the fact remains that people still create and operate the systems, making individual human development critical to any process of social improvement. This is taken for granted in Buddhist political thought.

Emphasis in Buddhism on individual liberation, even in schools whose express aim is collective liberation, has given rise to the misconception that it is a socially passive, even escapist, religion. While passivism and escapism are well-documented corruptions of certain practices, these attitudes are far from the spirit of Buddhism. Importance is placed on the commonweal even in the schools that focus primarily on individual liberation; the liberation of individuals is seen as an integral part of the welfare of society, reducing sources of conflict and enabling people to work for the benefit of others unhindered by personal ambition.

According to Buddhist teaching, even a simple act of generosity is not really genuine as long as it is tainted by personal feelings, even the desire to give or the satisfaction of giving. This does not mean that Buddhists withhold social action until they reach the ultimate objectivity, but that they do not use social action to mollify their own personal human feelings. Rather, Buddhists use action as a means of knowledge, and use knowledge to guide action. According to "The Book on the Ten Stages" in *The Flower Ornament Scripture*, one of the seminal texts of universalist Buddhism, when practitioners reach the stage where they are perfecting meditation, they "practice whatever in the world would benefit sentient beings." Among the activities mentioned in the scripture are writing, teaching, mathematics, natural science, medicine, performing arts, engineering, horticulture, and psychology.

History shows traces of Buddhist activity in a wide variety of cultural, social, economic, and political operations in Asia. Buddhist contributions to fine and applied arts, literature, philosophy, medicine, and education are comparatively well known. Buddhists also played an important part in reclamation and conservation of land, water, and human resources, as well as in the development of banking, trade, crafts, hostelry, communications, printing, and publishing. Buddhists participated in government at all levels, particularly local administration, but they also intervened from outside, sometimes arranging mass amnesties for political prisoners and even leading armed uprisings against oppressive regimes. Buddhism also established a socially acceptable means whereby women could exercise the right to divorce, as well as the first public facilities for orphans in the clan-oriented societies of old Asia.

The social activities of Buddhists of the past are not always noticed by Western observers who expect such activities to be invariably accompanied by a great deal of publicity as well as the constitution of official or quasi-official institutes and organizations for the discharge of these functions. Buddhism, in its purest sense, is based on the fluidity of events, and its programs are local and specific even if they are based on universal principles or a higher understanding of humanity. Zen Buddhism is particularly strident in its warnings against trying to institutionalize the "good" or the "holy" because of the sentimental attachments built up around these ideas, and the hypocrisy that feeds on these attachments.

Buddhism confronts the individual and society as a whole with the problems of self and mind, and does not allow for escapism— whether that escapism be by nihilism and quietism, or by immersion in movements that provide people with ready-made ideas, activities, and interests in which the devotee can "forget the self." Buddhist literature contains many warnings about the seductive delusions presented by these attempts to avoid the questions of self, mind, and true reality. Yet it is precisely these forms of escapism which because of their conspicuous nature are often mistaken for legitimate expressions of Buddhism and not recognized as deviations.

The first step of the Buddhist approach to liberation is to determine the source of bondage. According to a Zen proverb, "The answer is in the question," and the art of useful questioning is a key to Zen. The proverb also says, however, "The question is in the answer," in that it is not enough to know the answer, it is essential to work the answer out in life; thus the question becomes how to apply the answer to living situations.

The opening statement of the *Dhammapada*, perhaps the oldest written record of Buddha's teaching, provides a classic presentation of the problem of bondage, in which the answer and the question clearly contain each other. "Everything is based on mind, is lead by mind, is fashioned by mind. If you speak and act with a polluted mind, suffering will follow you, as the wheels of an oxcart follow the footsteps of the ox. Everything is based on mind, is lead by mind, is fashioned by mind. If you speak and act with a pure mind, happiness will follow you, as a shadow clings to a form."

Pursuing this basic theme, *The Flower Ornament Scripture*, the most comprehensive of Buddhist texts, says, "Mind is like an artist, able to paint the worlds." Contrasting the possibilities of mentally fashioned worlds, the scripture also says, "Some lands have no light; they are dark and full of fear, with pains like the wounds of weapons. Those who see them suffer by themselves. . . . Some worlds are terrifying, with great howls of pain, those voices most bitter and harsh, frightening all who hear. . . . In some lands are always heard heavenly sounds of various gods, pure sounds of celestial realms, or the voices of leaders of the worlds."

In a more detailed analysis of the root of involution, the "Ten Stages" book of *The Flower Ornament Scripture* says,

> Because of continually slipping into erroneous views, because
> of minds shrouded by the darkness of ignorance, because of
> being puffed up with pride, because of conceptions, because
> of mental fixations of desires caught in the net of craving,
> because of hopes pursued by actions in the tangle of deceit
> and falsehood, because of deeds connected with envy and
> jealousy producing mundane states, because of accumulation
> of actions rife with passion, hatred, and folly, because of the

flames of mind bound up with delusion, because of seeds in
the mind, intellect, and consciousness bound to the flows of
lust, existence, and ignorance, therefore ignorant people produce sprouts of subsequent life in the world.

Over the course of centuries, Zen developed a science of freedom,
dealing with both the subtle but knowable and coarse but ignorable
psychological bases of limitation and growth. This science was not a
new creation of Zen schools, however, for Zen inherited extremely
rich amalgams of Indian, central Asian, and Southeast Asian developments in the search for mental freedom. According to conditions,
however, the science of liberation always remained esoteric to a greater
or lesser degree, for three main reasons: first, because it is by its very
nature difficult for the conditioned mind to grasp; second, because of
the possibility of misuse; and third, because it was inevitably perceived
as a threat by people with proprietary interests in ideology and
custom, who naturally had considerable influence in society.

In accordance with tradition, generations of early Zen teachers
reexamined the principles and practices of this science and encoded it
in an immense body of anecdotes, aphorisms, and poetry, all designed
to protect the science and reproduce its desired effect, mental freedom.
In reality, there is some Zen in all schools of Buddhism, and there is
something of all schools of Buddhism to be found in Zen; in spite of
vast theoretical and methodological differences, where the aim of
freedom is realized there can be no difference in essence.

The basis for the symbolic Zen language of mind was constructed
within three or four centuries of the beginning of Zen in China.
During this time, many of the fundamental teachings and approaches
of Zen were put into groups of stories about the early masters. There
is, for example, the figure of the unfathomable Baozhi, a mendicant
meditation master of extraordinary attainments who taught mainly by
symbolic acts and laconic statements, which led to his being now
imprisoned for "disturbing the masses" with his miraculous powers,
now invited to court to enlighten the emperor. He is one of the first
adepts to leave writings prized in the Zen traditions.

Then there is the story of Fu Shanhui, a small farmer and family
man who by dint of his own study and effort attained higher consciousness and became a renowned philanthropist, teacher, and social
activist. He is known for converting many of his relatives and people

of his locality, and for his extraordinary acts of charity. He even tried to gain an interview with the emperor to offer him some advice on ameliorating the wretched conditions of the times, but because of his low social status he was unable to make any headway until Baozhi, who knew of Shanhui's enlightenment, intervened at court.

Both of these characters, Baozhi and Fu Shanhui, figure prominently in Zen lore; neither belonged to any perceptible school, but both represent prototypes of freedom and independence. Even the radical differences between them are typical of Zen, for as the saying goes, "If all the waves of the Zen stream were alike, innumerable ordinary people would get bogged down."

Both Baozhi and Fu Shanhui are said to have met Bodhidharma, who is usually called the founder of Zen and is one of the most important symbols of Zen tradition. Bodhidharma is represented as an Indian prince (like Buddha himself) who abandoned a life of luxury in order to seek a more permanent reality. According to the legend, his teacher was the leading Buddhist master in India of that time. This teacher instructed Bodhidharma to go to China sixty-seven years after the teacher's death, the story goes, so he traveled by the sea route from south India to China in his old age to carry out his mission.

Bodhidharma is represented as having drawn the distinction between sociocultural manifestations of religion and the ultimate understanding of Zen. To cross the broad cultural gap between India and China, Bodhidharma used the Buddhist doctrine of consciousness, which cuts through cultural and historical differences to the essence of the human mind. Much later, his teaching was referred to as "direct pointing to the human mind to see its essence and attain enlightenment."

The doctrine of consciousness is a useful tool for understanding what Zen does, and this is one reason for its traditional association with the Zen founder Bodhidharma. According to this teaching, things have three natures: imaginary, relative, and absolute. The essence and practice of Zen lie in these three natures and their interplay.

The imaginary nature of things means things as we conceive of them, as we represent them to ourselves subjectively. The imaginary nature of things is known by the way we think and talk about things. Thus the imaginary nature of things is conditioned by cultural and personal history and custom.

The relative nature of things is the nature of phenomena as

existing only in relation to one another. According to the doctrine, the inherent reality of this continuous interaction of interdependent conditions is ultimately beyond the scope of human conception, because all conceptions of it are mental images superimposed on it, not the thing in itself.

The absolute reality, the doctrine concludes, is the emptiness of reality, or the ultimate unreality, of the imaginary nature of things. It may also be described as the relative nature of things being empty of real correspondence to their imagined natures. The classical Zen master Baizhang said, "If you realize there is no connection between your senses and the external world, you will be liberated on the spot."

The doctrine says that absolute reality can be witnessed, but not by ordinary sense or thought. According to Buddhist texts that analyze the reception of Buddhism in human communities, when the doctrine is stated this far, there inevitably arises the idea that the aim of Buddhism is to depart from the fiction of imaginary reality to unite with the ultimate nature of absolute reality. According to these diagnostic texts, this misunderstanding is one of the main problems of practical Buddhism. It is dealt with very frequently in Zen writings.

According to the doctrine of consciousness, the imaginary reality of the present becomes incorporated into the available dimension of the relative reality of the future. In ordinary terms, views and attitudes condition deeds that influence environments, which in turn affect views and attitudes. The purpose of realization of absolute reality is not to annihilate imaginary reality but to attain the practical freedom to affect it deliberately, not just reinforce it by automatic habit.

The *Sandhinirmocana-sutra*, a classic of the consciousness-only doctrine, says that the essential means by which absolute reality is known is nonattachment to the imaginary reality. The Zen teachings of "mindlessness," "no thought," "stopping the mind," and so on, are all representations of this exercise of letting go of the image of the world to witness the absolute. This is why making the mind blank is rejected in Zen, since this state is just another image and not detachment from imagination.

One of the early classical Zen masters is often quoted as teaching this formula for Zen: "First you go over to the other side (the absolute) to find out it exists, then you come back to this side (the relative as it is perceived in common) to act." After a certain degree of experience, direct knowledge of absolute reality replaces meditation as the means to control one's relationship to imaginary reality.

Using the freedom this brings, the Zen Buddhist can then gain access to a greater range of consciousness of relative reality than is permitted by a closed system of attitudes and concepts. This increases potential for effective cultivation or reconstruction of imaginary reality in ways that will bring about improvements in future relative reality.

In the Flower Ornament School of Buddhism, from which Zen freely borrowed, this two-sided process is referred to in terms of "returning objects to mind" (realizing images are mental) and "realizing true emptiness" (fictional nature of images), then "projecting objects from mind" (working out viable, constructive images) and "realizing subtle being" (the concretization of thought in action).

Both of these steps have specific practical guidelines, or natural laws for working with the absolute and the relative. These are presented in many different ways throughout the Buddhist canon. One of the most explicit descriptions of the rule for the absolute, one that clarifies a basic attribute of Zen, is to be found in the *Sandhinirmocana-sutra*. According to this scripture the Buddha said,

> The ultimate truth of which I speak is that which is inwardly realized by sages, while the scope of thought and deliberation is what unenlightened people testify to among themselves. Therefore you should know that ultimate truth transcends all objects of thought and deliberation. The ultimate truth of which I speak has no form to which to relate, whereas thought and deliberation operate only in the sphere of forms. Therefore you should know that ultimate truth transcends all objects of thought and deliberation. The ultimate truth of which I speak cannot be expressed in words, whereas thought and deliberation only operate in the realm of verbalization. Therefore you should know that ultimate truth transcends all objects of thought and deliberation. The ultimate truth of which I speak has no representation, whereas thought and deliberation only operate in the realm of representation. Therefore you should know that ultimate truth transcends all objects of thought and deliberation. The ultimate truth of which I speak puts an end to all controversy, whereas thought and deliberation only operate in the realm of controversy. Therefore you should know that ultimate truth transcends all objects of thought and deliberation.

Thus classical Zen teachers insist that Zen cannot be understood or attained by ordinary cognition. The scripture goes on to illustrate how mental habits inhibit the awakening of the subtle formless perception and knowledge activated in Zen realization:

> Someone accustomed to pungent and bitter flavors all his life cannot think of or assess or believe in the sweetness of honey or sugar. Someone who in ignorance takes an overwhelming interest in desires because of passionate craving and is therefore inflamed with excitement, as a result, cannot think of or assess or believe in the marvelous bliss of detachment and inward effacement of sense data. Someone in ignorance who, because of overwhelming interest in words, clings to rhetoric, cannot, as a result, think of or assess or believe in the pleasure of holy silence with inner tranquillity. Someone in ignorance who, because of overwhelming interest in perceptual and cognitive signs, clings to the appearances of the world, cannot, as a result, think of or assess or believe in ultimate nirvana that obliterates all signs so that reification ends.
>
> Just as people in ignorance, because of their various controversies and beliefs involving attachments to self and possessions, cling to mundane contentions and therefore cannot think of or assess or believe in an ideal state in which there is no egotism, no possessiveness, no attachment, and no contention, in the same way those who pursue thoughts cannot think of or assess or believe in the character of the ultimate truth that is beyond the sphere of all thought and deliberation.

Because of the radical difference between Zen knowledge and ordinary knowledge, the emphasis placed on this absolute law in Zen teaching often draws so much attention that an imbalance is created. Nevertheless, in spite of the drawbacks of emphasizing the absolute—drawbacks mainly deriving from exaggerated reactions such as irrational yearning or fear—it is axiomatic that the relative rule itself cannot be made fully effective without realization of the absolute. Zen proverb says, "Let go over a cliff, die completely, and then come back to life—after that you cannot be deceived." Knowledge of the absolute is thus used to cut through subjective illusions or sentiments about what is indicated, or what is possible, in the realms of the relative and imaginary rules.

Perhaps the most concise yet inclusive definition of the relative rule—which is relative to the realm in which it is carried out—is articulated in the *Flower Ornament Scripture:* the rule states that enlightening action includes all "that which is conducive to the benefit and well being of all creatures." The steps taken to carry out this rule are summarized in two classical Zen stories: two masters were asked what one should do in daily life; one said, "I do not ask about daily life, I only require that your vision be true," and the other said, "Each step should tread on this question." Together these stories illustrate the harmonization of the two facets of Zen realization, following the traditional approach that avoids both dogma and denial.

One of the greatest tasks of Zen, therefore, is to make the transition between the imagined, relative, and absolute levels of reality as fluid as possible. The doctrine of consciousness uses another model for this purpose, that of "three subtle and six coarse aspects" of conscious representation. An excellent tool for self-observation, this model is also useful for understanding the purposes of Zen procedures.

The first of the three subtle aspects is called ignorant conditioned consciousness. This gives rise to what is called the state of excitement, which is the appearance of subjectivity. This second aspect produces the third, which is the objectivization of the views of this subjective state of excitement. Herein lies the imperceptible link between the relative and the imaginary. The appearance of the objectivization of subjectivity is further subjected to the treatment known as the six coarse aspects of consciousness.

The first of these six coarse aspects of consciousness is cognition, cognition of the characteristics of the mental constructs projected to define the world. The second aspect is continuity, or repetition of these constructs. The third is attachment to the specific appearances thus construed. The fourth coarse aspect of consciousness is assignment of labels. The fifth is action based on the ideas and attitudes thus engendered. The sixth and final aspect of conditioned consciousness is that of the pain caused by bondage to habit.

There are various Zen techniques used to interrupt the mental formation of vicious cycles at critical points in this chain of subtle and coarse aspects of conditioning. The stories and images of Zen tradition are themselves means of affecting the quality of consciousness by their impact on certan links of the chain.

Bodhidharma is said to have founded Zen in China based on the doctrine of consciousness without any organizational ties. According to one legend, Bodhidharma spent over fifty years in China, teaching whenever the occasion arose. Other sources say he was there for a much briefer period and was much more limited in his activity. It is generally believed that he communicated the innermost secrets of Zen to four people, including one woman. It is also said that he was poisoned six times by rivalrous Buddhist priests, and finally allowed himself to die, at a very advanced age, when his teaching mission was completed.

As so often happens in Zen tradition, most of Bodhidharma's heirs disappear from center stage into the historical unknown. Most of the lore of later generations focuses on only one of the first Chinese Zen masters, a man named Huike. There are several key stories about Huike, representing such topics as the triumph of mind over matter, the Zen exercise of looking for the source of mind, the use of hectic environments to test mental stability, and the continuity of Zen work in the midst of ordinary work. Huike used to go to the outer gates of great urban monasteries and give talks on the formless teaching of Zen mind, drawing large crowds. As a result, like Bodhidharma he was persecuted by sectarians, finally to die by execution at a very advanced age.

Three hundred years later, a famous Zen master was to say, "Our ancestors were driven out wherever they went," referring to the psychological reality that the radical independence of Zen is anathema to ordinary human sentiment, leaving the individual with the solitary struggle of lifting sensibility above the rationalization and emotion that regard familiarity as the fundamental criterion of reality.

Huike is said to have had ten private students, nearly half of them lay people, to whom he communicated the essence of Zen. In view of the intensity and weight of the illustrative tales of early Zen, concentrating whole lifetimes and generations into a few vignettes, it is noteworthy that this lore claims that women and lay people were included in Zen Buddhism from its very inception.

Very many Buddhist scriptures and other writings are regularly addressed to lay men and women, and contain many examples of male and female lay adepts and teachers. Zen history also says that the lineages of the so-called Five Houses of Zen, the major classical schools of Zen in China, were all patched by women at critical junctures during their formative generations.

The prospect of liberation for women and the common person in general was, as usual, regarded by entrenched political interests as a threat to the constituted order of society. This was a major reason why mendicants, who in their true form were people who had abandoned personal interest in wordly gain or loss, were commonly chosen to represent Buddhism publicly, in order to calm the irrational fears of politicians and academics. When some monks became potentates themselves, however, and politics invaded the monasteries, this particular function diminished accordingly.

Zen master Huike is also represented as caring for the sick, part of the overall tradition of Buddhist practice. His most famous healing was of Sengcan, a man with a dreaded disease who was eventually to become Huike's Zen successor. In this case Huike is said to have used purely spiritual means of healing to release the hold of the illness on the man and enable him to recover his health naturally and spontaneously.

Mental healing in Zen, important enough to be included among the tales of the founders, appears here and there throughout Zen history but is seldom singled out for emphasis. The mental healing of Huisi, another early Zen master reckoned as one of the founders of Tiantai Buddhism, is also documented in Zen history. His student Zhiyi, the definitive author of the highly articulated Tiantai system of Buddhism, included teachings on healing methods in his famous works on meditation.

Huike's successor Sengcan, is traditionally credited with authorship of "The Trusting Heart," one of the earliest and most enduringly popular works on Zen. Quotations from this favorite work appear throughout later Zen literature. Generally speaking, it is a guide to Zen meditation, but the unifying theme is mental balance. Many of the Zen instructions translated in the present volume are very much in the spirit of this early Zen classic.

Sengcan's successor Daoxin was the first great Chinese Zen master to establish a special commune for intensive Zen study. Like numerous other Zen masters, he is represented as refusing the honors bestowed on him by the emperor of China, illustrating the transcendence of Zen over wordly ambitions.

Now that Zen was in the public eye, Daoxin articulated a wide variety of methods and strictly exacting criteria for Zen teachers. He emphasized the natural law of Zen transmission, that no one could possibly teach Zen to another without having already attained perfect clarity of mind. He himself is said to have given only one of five hundred students permission to teach. This student, a man of unknown origin named Hongren, attracted a following of seven hundred students, eleven of whom became recognized as enlightened successors and public Zen teachers.

Hongren is formally designated as the author of a short treatise on the Zen technique of preserving the original mind, but this work is little noted in Zen tradition. More commonly Hongren is associated with the transcendent wisdom teaching of Buddhism, which distinguishes mind from mental states and separates the essence of religion from emotion and sentimentality. The transcendent wisdom teaching, also central to Tiantai Buddhist praxis, came to be used in Zen schools to such an extent that some observers have identified Zen with a development of this particular phase of Buddhism.

With the career of Hongren's foremost successor, the renowned Zen master Huineng, the history of what shortly became the mainstream of Zen began. Huineng, who died in the early eighth century, is portrayed as an illiterate young woodcutter from a backward region of China who suddenly awoke to the truth of Zen when he happened to hear someone reciting a popular transcendent wisdom scripture. According to legend, he stayed in the community of the great Zen master Hongren for a brief time as manual laborer, received recognition of his enlightenment, then fled in secret to avoid the hostility of the scholars in the community. He spent fifteen years living in the mountains with bands of hunters, and finally reappeared in southern China as a mature Zen master who attracted seekers of truth from all over China.

The legend of Huineng typifies a number of basic Zen themes. Being from a backward area, without social status or formal education, he represents the same transcendence of caste and custom that the original Buddha represented when he declared the ancient Indian caste system invalid in Buddhism and told people not to believe in anything just because it is a traditional belief, or because it is written in books or pronounced by authorities. And just as Buddhism produced the first great sacred Indian literature in vernacular languages, so did Zen Buddhism produce, in the three centuries after Huineng, a sacred literature in vernacular Chinese.

Enlightened as a young man without the benefit of any previous training or education, Huineng responded to a test devised by Hongren to illustrate something to his large community of students. Zen tradition represents these students as highly learned and well-trained Buddhist monks—and history affirms that many such advanced Buddhists of other schools flocked to Zen in its early centuries. The young, uninitiated but enlightened Huineng is portrayed as surpassing even the greatest of these distinguished scholars and practitioners, with the supreme wisdom known as teacherless knowledge.

Throughout mainstream Zen there is the idea that Zen understanding may be provoked by cultivation, but no amount of deliberate cultivation can absolutely guarantee Zen realization. There is, according to tradition, an indefinable element necessary to potentiate the Zen effect. This is a thing that is not a thing, the ineffable wisdom called teacherless knowledge. This is held to be inherent in everyone, but Huineng is especially singled out as the master of teacherless knowledge to show how enlightenment does not depend on conditioning.

This independent knowledge is also called "the subtlety that cannot be passed on, even from father to son." It is not like ritual transmission of formal knowledge or authority, nor like a doctrine or creed. Several of the classical masters are most emphatic on this point, and one of the major controversies of Zen history was in effect caused by people who denied the necessity of enlightenment on one's own but claimed there was a secret transmission. The medium of this "secret transmission" naturally became contaminated with personal views, and then with personal feelings.

The legendary attack of one faction of monks against Huineng is a classic model of what happens when proprietary feelings attach themselves to religion. From the very beginning of Zen when the founder Bodhidharma told the emperor of China his pious acts had no merit, through the ages Zen has dealt with this problem of ulterior egoism in religion. According to a Zen proverb, "If you have no feelings about wordly things, they are all Buddhism; if you have feelings about Buddhism, it is a wordly thing."

According to traditional Zen history, Huineng had thirty-three enlightened disciples who became local teachers, while "the others who hid their names and concealed their tracks could not all be counted." This also becomes a recurring theme in Zen lore, where people who come to understand Zen disappear into the fabric, while only a few appear to continue the public teaching of Zen. In China, at least, this was matched in concrete history by a virtually continuous scattering and reformation of Zen schools, and by the emergence of successive phases of Zen teaching under different names in different guises.

After the completion of Huineng's teaching and the dismantling of his school, Zen quietly and informally penetrated the ancient Buddhist establishments, then burst into bloom under the guidance of two extraordinary Zen masters of the eighth century, Shitou and Mazu. These two teachers, known as "the two doors of immortality," and almost all of the known Zen masters of the following generation were taught by both of them.

Shitou, whose lifetime spanned nearly the entire eighth century, is particularly well known for his remarkable didactic poem entitled "Merging of Difference and Sameness." This is one of the most compact statements of Buddhism on record, written at a high level of concentration. Many attempts have been made to elucidate its inner meanings, with commentaries dating all the way back to the late classical period of Zen, only a few generations removed from the original composition.

In the typical manner of texts written in a concentrated Zen style, Shitou's work says a great deal about the fundamental premises of Zen right in the opening statement: "The mind of the great immortal of India is intimately communicated East and West." The great immortal of India refers to Buddha, and that mind refers to the enlightened mind. The term used for immortal here is a Taoist term, and the characters in the title of the work are identical to an early Taoist classic of spiritual alchemy. Here Shitou is not just using literary embellishment or approximation of concepts; the message is that the enlightened mind cuts through and goes beyond distinctions of religious format, is deeper than and unimpeded by cultural differences such as those between East and West.

Shitou's great contemporary Mazu, whose lifetime also spanned nearly the entire eighth century, is the first of the Zen masters whose instructions are translated in this volume. Most of what is known about Mazu is to be found in the records of his interactions with other people, recounting tales of sudden awakenings said to have been provoked by his words, acts, and charismatic influence. Mazu had one hundred and thirty-nine enlightened disciples, eighty-four of whom became public teachers. His spiritual descendants created a major impact over the next few hundred years.

Mazu's recorded teaching is extremely simple yet encompassing, emphasizing psychological normalcy in the Zen sense of freedom from the fluctuation of mental contrivances and artificialities. To accomplish or restore this normalcy, Mazu taught people not to cling to subjective views; by this means, he claimed, it is possible to transcend the ordinary world without isolation or rejection of everyday life. Mazu said that thoughts and feelings congeal over individual and cultural lifetimes, forming the substance of the apparent world.

His basic Zen technique involved using this realization to impersonalize oneself and society, relaxing the grip of mind on its creations and letting go of thought trains, thus arriving at an inconceivable perception of reality. According to Mazu, enlightenment means realization of the essence of mind and objects, and its fruition is beyond the practices that lead to its attainment.

One of Mazu's many outstanding spiritual heirs was Dazhu, whose sayings follow those of Mazu in this collection. Dazhu presents a prime example of the profound simplicity of this early Zen. He elucidates the shortcoming of the religious ego or religious passion so typically criticized in later Zen writings; making a business of Buddhist studies, Dazhu says, may incapacitate people for authentic experience of liberation, insofar as studies are pursued in a frame of mind affected by ordinary subjectivity and object-fascination.

In somewhat later times, when Zen was even more well established, teachers often noted links between sterile approaches to Zen and ordinary material greed, as Zen communes were transformed into wordly institutions and walks of life, complete with social and material systems of rewards and punishments, bailiwicks, factions, and all that proceeds from them. The roots of this problem, however, were already articulated in the early generations of Zen Buddhism by Dazhu and other successors of Mazu's school.

The next Zen master whose instructions appear in this volume is Linji, a redoubtable teacher of the ninth century. Taught by a spontaneously enlightened man who had also associated with Baizhang, one of Mazu's outstanding disciples, Linji consummated the structural representation of the Zen teaching that had come down to him, and brought it to life with his own extraordinary enlightenment. The record of his sayings, originally compiled by an immediate disciple, became one of the outstanding classics of Zen. It is from this famous record that the selections here are translated.

Like other Zen masters teaching normalcy, Linji warned students not to seek extraordinary powers. He did not deny such powers, but implied that subjective imaginations and personal desires were not sound bases for developing the higher potentials of mind. Linji insisted that what people really need is true perception and understanding; attain this, he said, and wonders come of themselves. He emphasized the importance of independence, refusing to take on other's confusions and delusions, trusting in the innermost self. Linji told people to do whatever they had to do, without being changed by external influences.

Like other Zen masters, Linji referred to Zen as the teaching of the mind ground, the most fundamental level of awareness. He taught that the mind ground can go freely into both sacred and profane realms without being identified with either. Be independent, he said, not dwelling even on the mind ground, not leaning on either internal states or external conditions; then situations that arise cannot change you, and this radical independence releases you even from vicious habits.

Linji also warned that indiscriminate study is ineffective, likening it to a goat nosing around and chewing on whatever it finds. Special discernments are essential if study is to progress beyond a certain point, he explained; professional religionists who cannot distinguish obsession from enlightenment consequently form what are in effect social organizations rather than spiritual bodies. This is not independence in the Zen sense of the word. As Linji says, "If you love the scared and despise the ordinary, you are still bobbing in the ocean of delusion."

Linji taught that mental blocks hindering both spiritual as well as social life are caused by clinging to labels and slogans. These mental blocks inhibit perception of objective truth, he said, by trapping the mind within the walls of ideas and attitudes continually reinforced by what the doctrine of consciousness calls "the lull of words." To be free from such influences, Linji insisted, it is imperative to know the real self; but this real self cannot be deliberately sought, because the deliberation is already artificial. Herein lies the subtlety of Zen.

According to the history as described by Zen masters, the subtlety of Zen, of its very nature impossible to grasp by the ordinary intellect, was eventually used as a veil by meddlers, charlatans, and would-be teachers fascinated by the power of mystification. According to Linji, many Zennists who are not really enlightened climb to the position of teachers as an anticipated career step. Imposters hide behind mysterious sayings or ritualized religiosity. Pious but naive people may be deceived by pretenders of this sort, whose "teaching" is not liberative but is, on the contrary, binding. Again like many other authentic masters, Linji speaks out clearly against false Zen transmitters, showing how to recognize and avoid the aggressive mental suggestion of imitation Zen.

Like the Buddha, Linji maintains that to attain liberation it is necessary to detach emotion and intellect from preconceptions formed by social conditioning, including traditional and religious beliefs, in order to recover the mental spaciousness and objectivity needed for a universal perspective on reality. Typically, in this connection Linji asserts that there is no doctrine in Zen, because Zen is just a matter of "curing ailments and unlocking fetters."

Following Linji in this volume are sayings of his contemporary Yangshan. Yangshan was noted as one of the great geniuses of Zen, and many high officials called themselves his disciples. Numerous anecdotes of Yangshan are found in standard collections of Zen stories. Yangshan is noted for emphasizing the nondogmatic nature of Zen teaching, which operates by response to need rather than by profession and assertion. Yangshan stated that absolute Zen is beyond human feeling and does not appeal to the sensation seeker.

This perspective is itself sometimes regarded as dogmatic by people who are accustomed to dogma, but the inaccessibility of absolute Zen to ordinary thought and feeling is not considered by Buddhists to be a doctrine but a quality of its inherent nature, as explained in the *Sandhinirmocana-sutra*.

Like Linji, Yangshan warned people not to seek the miraculous but to get at the essential, the basic true mind; all marvels are outgrowths, he said, which come of themselves when the basis is established. Subjective attraction to the unusual or extraordinary is not regarded as a sound basis for Zen practice, since it still imprisons the mind within its own images. This does not mean that Zen masters do not develop extraordinary capacities, only that they do not strive for them for their own sake.

The next Zen master presented in this collection is Fayan, who died in the mid-tenth century. Fayan was the last of the great classical masters whose schools perfected the early articulation of Buddhism in Zen terms. His school, particularly known for its demonstration of what Zen scholarship is and how it functions, had an especially great impact on Korea during its first three generations. One of Fayan's successors was instrumental in reviving the ancient Tiantai school of Buddhism. Among the latter's heirs was the ninth patriarch of Pure Land Buddhism, a master of Zen and all the schools, pioneer of a new pan-Buddhist movement.

Fayan himself is mainly known for teaching advanced students, but he also wrote a succinct treatise on general guidelines for Zen schools, criticizing the decadent trends he observed in Zen sects even at that time, and plainly outlining the true ideals of Zen. In this Fayan continued and further articulated a critical tradition that is strongly marked in the teachings of the successors and descendants of Mazu and was to become highly intensified in Zen as taught during the Song dynasty (960-1278), when Zen influence on Chinese culture was paramount. The selections translated here are from this treatise, one of the earliest Zen writings.

The first point Fayan made in his guidelines is the need to be enlightened oneself before teaching others. He wrote that degeneration in Zen was caused by people seeking to become Zen teachers and group leaders. It is therefore imperative, he taught, to clarify the basis of mind and detach oneself from vicious cycles that imprison the attention and perception within artificially conditioned limitations. Fayan also said that true Zen clarity and enlightenment cannot be accomplished by meditation without correct guidance.

Among the deteriorations in Zen schools to which Fayan's treatise makes special reference is sectarianism. Fayan wrote that while Zen has no sectarian ways to value, eventually followers became traditionalistic, sectarian, and competitive. To counteract this tendency, Fayan taught people not to simply memorize slogans and not to just follow the format of a school in the manner of political stooges following a party line. As models of the true approach to Zen, Fayan's treatise cites some of the famous sayings of earlier masters in this regard, saying, "The secret is in you," and "Everything flows from your own heart."

Fayan also warned people not to mistake impermanent states for real attainments, and not to allow theory and practice, or principle and fact, to become alienated from one another. The misperception of cultivated states as enlightenment experiences is rather typical of deteriorated Zen schools with a taste for excitement, while the alienation of theory and practice is typical of doctrinal schools using standardized systems. Both of these extremes are well documented in Zen diagnostic lore, as is the subjective interpretation of Zen stories, another common deterioration also condemned by Fayan in his treatise.

These translations from the sayings and writings of the classical masters Mazu, Dazhu, Linji, Yangshan, and Fayan are followed by selections from the writings of two pioneers in the literary projection of Zen during the tenth and eleventh centuries, Fenyang and Xuedou, and sayings of two teaching masters who accelerated the mid-Song dynasty development of Zen, Huanglong and Yangqi.

The literary projection of Zen was instrumental in penetrating the general fabric of Chinese and Chinese-influenced cultures and societies, but it only represents one part of the total impact of Zen. Fenyang and Xuedou were also successful teachers as well as exceptionally talented writers, but their contribution to Zen literature stands out most prominently. Fenyang had met more than seventy Zen masters, and incorporated the teachings of all the major lines of Zen into his writings, also adding his own comments and creating new forms of ancient Zen linguistic devices.

Fenyang emphasized the basic Buddhist idea that enlightenment is inherent in the mind but is obscured by acquired habits of perception and thought. Delusion and enlightenment are both rooted in the mind, Fenyang writes, but most people do not really take the idea of inherent buddha-nature seriously because they are wrapped up in personal thoughts, feelings, and moods. This is the reason for the existence of Zen teaching in spite of the fact that it is ultimately imperative, as Fenyang says, to "know for yourself."

According to Fenyang, although Zen teaching is impersonal, it needs the affinity or attunement of the seeker with Zen itself. The relationship between Zen teacher and apprentice is critical, but it is not the same as the relationship between teacher and student in conventional systems of education, particularly in that Zen cannot be fully explained or conveyed in ordinary terms. As Fenyang says, a thousand books are not enough, yet even one word is too much.

Furthermore, Zen education is distinguished from ordinary

learning in that competition, a well-recognized element of conventional systems, only wastes time in Zen. While Zen awakening is key to peace of mind in the midst of the world and unlocks hidden capacities, the freedom of Zen is not useful for the unprepared. Thus Zen education places extraordinarily high levels of responsibility on both teachers and students, requiring what is from the point of view of secular schools an unusual degree of maturity.

Xuedou is considered the reviver of what was perhaps the most arcane and elaborate of the classical schools of Zen, which employed techniques that had always required special genius. He is particularly noted for three outstanding literary works: a collection of verses on one hundred Zen stories, a collection of prose comments on another set of one hundred Zen stories, and an anthology of poetry. His living successors also grew into one of the most powerful schools of Zen during the late Song dynasty, and his writings even influenced the early Complete Reality School of Taoism.

Xuedou wrote that the living meaning of Zen is the design of life itself, and that really intimate understanding cannot be obtained from another person. This principle of Zen—that it is ultimately realized within oneself—also came to be used as a mask for all sorts of personalistic versions of Zen, but Xuedou warned that it is necessary to strip the mind of acquired illusions before seeing reality directly. This caveat is similar to that articulated by Fayan in regard to Zen stories, which he said required mental purification to understand and employ.

In contrast to Fenyang and Xuedou, Huanglong and Yangqi are examples of Zen masters who are famed mainly for the effects of their schools rather than for their literary remains, their own personal teachings being relatively little known. There is a collection of Huanglong's letters extant, but they are largely concerned with current events and seldom contain overt Zen instructions.

Analyzing the condition of bondage from which Zen proposes to liberate people, Huanglong uses a famous expression from Flower Ornament Buddhism: knowledge of reality is blocked by feelings, and things are shaped by images; people tend to fall into habits based on these feelings and images, and hence unconsciously bind themselves. To arrive at spontaneous Zen awakening for the solution of this problem, Huanglong continues, it is necessary to stop the restless mind. Going around to schools looking for teachers, he says, "busies you fatally."

According to Huanglong, the supreme Zen knowledge, knowledge that cannot be taught, is beyond ordinary intellectual exercise or study. The essence of Zen, he said, is beyond the material senses and cannot be reached by sensory experiences. This does not mean, however, that ordinary experience is to be avoided or rejected to seek Zen, for "Zen seekers should sit on the site of universal enlightenment right in the midst of all the thorny situations in life, and recognize their original face while mixing with the ordinary world." Freedom on earth, he taught, means to be ready for anything; people who are stuck in detachment and cannot enter the realm of passions unscathed can help neither themselves nor others.

Hardly anything is known of Yangqi, despite the fame of his school and the powerful influence of the line of teachers descended from him. Yangqi said that the condition of the environment depends on the individual and collective mentalities and actions of its inhabitants, but the individual and collective mentalities and actions of the inhabitants are also conditioned by the environment. From inside, this circle is the suffocating wheel of bondage itself, but with extradimensional consciousness able to deliberately transform thought and behavior it becomes a field of progressive action.

Detachment from the images formed by the process of conditioning, Yangqi said, undermines their spellbinding power and enables the mind to recover the autonomy that makes fresh progress possible. Nothing is destroyed by this experience, however, except the force of illusion; Yangqi taught that there is still human feeling, corresponding to the design and reason of the natural world.

Yangqi also said that there are ultimately no teachers of absolute Zen. When you understand Zen, he claimed, there is no more need for schools—you can go on your way freely, independent and whole. When the mind is "open and clear as space," he explained, the original intelligence is clear; and when consciousness is "broad and deep as the ocean," there is equanimity in the midst of events. In order to achieve this, he said, presence of mind in action is necessary.

The next four teachers appearing in this collection—Wuzu, Yuanwu, Foyan, and Dahui—were distinguished representatives of the so-called East Mountain School of Zen, which was descended from the classical master Linji through Yangqi. Noted for its great influence among the secular intelligentsia, the East Mountain School is among the most extensively documented branches of Zen.

Wuzu had already reached middle age when he entered Zen specialization under the tutelage of one of the Zen prodigies of the time, Baiyun, a direct heir of Yangqi who became a Zen teacher at an unusually young age and passed away early. Baiyun sent Wuzu to run the mill operated by the Zen monastery in a town below the mountain on which the monastery was located. It is said that whenever monks would come down the mountain snooping around, Wuzu would scandalize them by flirting with the young women who came to the mill.

Wuzu was later known for a skill in teaching that was unique in his time, using graphic stories, colorful metaphors, earthy poetry, profound abstractions, paradoxical actions, and forthright statements to open the minds of his hearers. Much of the dynamic of the East Mountain School's influence can be traced to the great capacity of Wuzu. He was outspoken in his criticism of the Zen institutions of his era, which he declared to have become infected by elements of human behavior inconsistent with the true aims and practices of Zen. Consequently he was also explicit in his descriptions of what he considered appropriate criteria for authentic Zen, for both the generalist and the specialist. His disciples and descendants in the East Mountain School followed him in this.

Wuzu made a point of the need for Zen guides to strip away even seekers' most cherished conceptions in order for them to reach the subtlety of Zen that cannot be categorized or defined in any conventional terms, cannot be imagined, and cannot be reached by thought. Later certain sayings of his were especially used for this purpose. But even this subtlety is not, he said, to be made into a "nest" in mature Zen, and it is not to be taken personally as an attainment—as the Zen proverb has it, "A general may establish peace, but it is not for the general to see peace."

Yuanwu, one of Wuzu's three most illustrious disciples, is distinguished as the author of *The Blue Cliff Record*, an outstanding Zen literary classic. There is also a large collection of records of his talks, verses on Zen subjects, and letters of Zen instruction. These letters of instruction, particularly esteemed by later students of Zen mind, were collected under the title "Essentials of Mind." It is from this famous text that the selections here are taken.

Yuanwu affirmed the expedient nature of Zen teachings and practices, which are not supposed to be fixed dogmas and rites, but means of helping people arrive at the source of mind and be free from illusions. Zen is in you, Yuanwu said; its penetrating insight and profound calm always exist. Look for the level of mind that is not dancing with objects and hanging around with things, he instructed; clear the mind, forget about subjective opinions and feelings, and you see what is meant by the Zen saying "Mind is Buddha."

Like his teacher Wuzu, Yuanwu was highly critical of deteriorated Zen studies. He noted that many intellectuals and educated people study Zen as a hobby and conversation piece. Zen was used as a status symbol and became the basis for a great deal of snobbery because of its honored position in Chinese culture. This kind of interest in Zen increases rather than decreases egotistic attachments. Thus Yuanwu insisted on the right purpose and inspiration for Zen study, particularly recommending the exercise of looking at death to clarify the will. Yuanwu also affirmed that quietude is not necessary for Zen study and practice—be empty inside while harmonizing with the environment, he said, and you will be at peace even in the midst of busy activity in the world.

Yuanwu explained that the changes made in Zen method over the ages by truly perceptive and free guides were needed to prevent people from clinging to outward faces of the teaching and rationalizing them into inflexible principles. "All of the teachings are expedients," he wrote, "just for the purpose of breaking through obsessions, doubts, intellectual interpretations, and egocentric ideas." This is of a different order from ritualistic sectarian cults claiming to be Zen schools in later times.

Yuanwu also affirmed that real Zen does not need social support and is not vulnerable to destructive social pressures. He explained both fallacies and realities of Zen, how to avoid the fallacies and how to usefully employ the realities. In these discussions he included remarks on such topics as the so-called living and dead word of Zen, the sterility of creeds, dogma, and slogans, and the need for balance in the types of techniques employed.

A basic aspect of this balance is summarized by Yuanwu in terms also familiar in Taoism: "If you want to attain intimate realization of Zen, first of all don't seek it. What is attained by seeking has already fallen into intellection. . . . Only when you stop your compulsive mind . . . do you pass through to freedom." He also quotes the ancient master Dazhu on the subject of external seeking: "Everything comes from your own heart. This is what an ancient called bringing out the family treasure."

In terms of method, Yuanwu taught people to still their thoughts, adding that "it is good to do this right in the midst of disturbance." He told people to let go of "previous imaginings, opinions, interpretations, wordly knowledge, intellectualizing, egoism, and competitiveness" to make the mind "clean and naked," thus to open up to Zen. After that, however, he said it is still necessary to develop consistency. For both stages he insisted on the importance of will, in that it requires extraordinary resolve to purify the heart and keep it clean, because one needs constant awareness of inner and outer states and actions. "Only those who have attained the fundamental," he wrote, "are capable of being inwardly empty while outwardly harmonious."

Detachment and cessation of thought are means, not ends, of Zen. Yuanwu said that when the process of Zen is consummated, "There are no mundane things outside Buddhism, and there is no Buddhism outside mundane things." After awakening to reality, he stated, "With every thought you are consulting infinite teachers."

If even deep meditations are only tools in Zen, how much the more so are words. They have enormous potential as expedient means of stimulating perceptions, but they are not liberative when transformed into totems. Yuanwu wrote that when you realize the verbal teachings of the enlightened are within you, "you do not wear them around on your head." He was constantly warning people about faddish and cultish behavior, which may provide some emotional satisfactions but does not produce Zen awakening.

Yuanwu also mentioned another specific abuse of artifacts like writings, well documented in Zen diagnostic lore, characterized by judgment of the artifacts in ordinary sentimental and intellectual terms based upon subjective comparisons. As tools, these writings are precision instruments designed to measure and to guide. Although one of their functions is to reveal defective or incomplete mentation, the value of this effect depends on other factors, such as the attitude of the individual. One of the persistent themes of Zen is to note imbalances and flaws in one's own mind and thought, in order to deliberately counterbalance or overcome them, and avoid their future appearance.

According to Yuanwu, thorough independence means that mindfulness and mindlessness leave no impression on your soul. Then even troublesome events do not affect your thoughts; you are inwardly serene while outwardly adaptable. Yuanwu also discussed Zen teacherhood, emphasizing compassion, tact, impartiality, being unobtrusive and noncompetitive. He added that opposition could cause no personal feelings, and followed the ancient Taoist teaching that "no one can contend with one who does not contend." Eventually, Yuanwu said, "malicious pests will disappear of themselves."

Yuanwu cautioned seekers that time and practice are needed to reach the possibilities indicated by Zen guides, and in this interval all sorts of false teachers may try to teach the uncertain. He described one major characteristic of spiritual charlatans as leading people into "fooling around with curios." In this respect real Zen teaching is anathema to religious cultists and literary dilettantes.

Explaining Zen teaching methods, Yuanwu said that devices of real Zen teachers are geared to "hook" people, or bring out their dominant confusion or controlling attitude, in order to liberate them from these limitations. Imagining these devices to represent the beliefs of the masters themselves, turning them into articles of faith or slogans of a school, results in the creation of ineffective and often thoroughly absurd interpretations of Zen teaching.

Yuanwu was one of the outstanding Zen masters commonly associated by historians with a watershed in the history of the use of Zen stories in the process of Zen learning and teaching. Although he said it was a serious mistake not to wonder about the sayings of the ancients after awakening oneself, thus taking advantage of the perceptual leverage they provide, he also said that the use of sayings and stories is not absolutely essential for some people: "Just correct your attention and quiet your mind from the time you arise in the morning, and whatever you say or do, review it carefully and see where it comes from and what makes it all happen."

Mind watching may itself become an unproductive and confusing activity without the detachment necessary to objectivity. Yuanwu stressed that it is not necessary to abandon action in the world in order to attain freedom. Stilling the mind, he taught, at best an expedient, may give the subjective impression of emptiness, but is not in itself the emptiness that Buddhism calls the ultimate truth. Real Zen emptiness, or openness, he said, is alive and cannot be pinned down; it is neither in being nor in nonbeing, it is beyond the attitudes of rejection or attachment. Eventually, Yuanwu wrote, "You can trust this true, pure ineffable mind, and when mundane conditions beckon involvement, you notice that the mind does not go along with them."

With Yuanwu, Zen master Foyan was one of the so-called "Three Buddhas" of the early East Mountain School under the tutelage of the great Wuzu. There is an immense record of his teachings, including one of the largest collections of direct instructions in the Zen canon. The selections translated in this volume are taken from these direct instructions, which utilize one of the most subtle forms of Zen wisdom.

Foyan taught people to detach from thought, an exercise that does not require stopping the mind but is used to achieve the same purpose. "We do not teach you to annihilate random thoughts, suppress body and mind, close your eyes, and consider this Zen," he said, stressing the importance of what he called "saving energy," effortlessly preserving the integrity of the original mind. Foyan also emphasized independence and self-observation, explaining that subjective feelings, or subjective interpretations of the objective world, are not themselves the real, objective world.

Foyan talks about a wide range of practical matters in a simple and straightforward manner that while easy to understand shows the true difficulty of Zen. "You must know how to check yourself before you can attain Zen," he said, illustrating a number of ways to approach this activity. One thing Foyan does not recommend is that confused people go rushing around looking for gurus when they should first be looking into where they became confused. Like other Zen masters, he says, "It is just a matter of reaching the source of mind."

The liberation proposed by Zen, realized by arriving at the source of mind, is not only liberation from unnecessary limitation and suffering, but liberation of a vast reserve of power inherent in reality. This is a very important point, connecting with Foyan's recurrent warning not to think that Zen involves suppression of mind and body. It is customary for Zen masters to refrain from discussing the higher powers latent in the human mind (although they are described at length in certain Buddhist texts), and to avoid making a display of such powers. This custom is observed to discourage people from seeking Zen for reasons of personal ambition, but it has also encouraged the mistaken identification of "normalcy" as understood in Zen with "normalcy" as defined in the terms accepted by social systems which do little or nothing to foster the development of human consciousness beyond the limits of those systems.

So useful did the Foyan's general talks prove to later seekers that they were collected into a book ranked among one of the three so-called incomparables of Zen literature. Another one of these three "incomparables" is the famous collection of the letters of Dahui, a successor of Yuanwu whose impact as a Zen teacher was so extraordinary that he is sometimes described as a reincarnation of Linji, the redoubtable spiritual ancestor of the whole East Mountain School of Zen. Selections from these letters follow Foyan's talks in the translations contained in this volume.

Dahui was particularly noted for his ability to explain Zen in plain terms, his extraordinary capabilities in provoking Zen awakening, and his practice of collecting rare and unusual Zen lore. While still in the circle of his teacher Yuanwu, Dahui was given the special assignment of dealing with the lay people who come seeking advice, and later as a teacher he also carried out extensive correspondence with lay seekers.

Dahui made extensive use of the teaching of *The Flower Ornament Scripture* and the meditation known as the "oceanic reflection," from which this scripture is said to derive. He stressed that buddhahood is not an externally perceptible form, but is an inner knowledge. Teaching the expedient of being like aware space, seeing Buddha everywhere in everything, Dahui stated that there is no need for the trappings of religion or spirituality in studying Zen. What is essential, he said, is awakeness; examine yourself, he taught, beware of distraction and partiality. Find out the source of mind, he continued, and when it is necessary to change things, do so by changing the mind. According to Dahui, impartiality is the true meaning of Zen "mindlessness," and this part of his teaching was incorporated verbatim into a secular handbook on civil service and statecraft.

Like Foyan and others, Dahui said that it is important not to abandon the ordinary world to study Zen. Many study Zen earnestly only when they have troubles, he observed, then slack off when they become successful in the world. For Zen enlightenment, he stated, it is not necessary to give up family and friends and retire from one's occupation, not necessary to be a vegetarian, an ascetic or an eremite. People who outwardly abandoned society while inwardly retaining ordinary sentiments were those who transformed Zen communities into families, societies, and occupations that may have differed from wordly organizations in external trappings and professed ideologies but nevertheless were based on a thoroughly worldly psychology.

Dahui said that teachers without enlightenment, careerists in monastic society, just make clones of themselves and do not communicate enlightenment. In this way the transformation of Zen into a mundane counterfeit proceeded apace during the Song dynasty, inspiring Dahui and others to come forth with their cutting criticism. According to the real adepts, reputed Zen masters and schools may in reality be creations of hobbyists who record and enshrine what they like. One of the telltale signs of self-deceived Zennists, however, is that they usually do not recognize real seers if they do happen to meet them, and even if they recognize them it is useless because the self-deceived are seeking agreement and approval, not understanding.

Zen master Hongzhi, a great contemporary of Dahui, was one of the last living representatives of his lineage of Zen, and is considered by some to have completed the articulation and refinement of the Song dynasty Zen literary project. Extracts from his Zen instructions are translated in this volume, following the selections from Dahui's letters.

Hongzhi made altogether extraordinary contributions to Zen literature in every form. His poetry is among the most refined work of its kind, and even his prose has a poetic quality that is rarely equaled. He compiled two famous collections of one hundred Zen stories each, adding his own comments, one set in poetry and the other in prose, paralleling those of the earlier Xuedou. There is also a considerable collection of Hongzhi's other talks, sayings, poems, and writings. Translated here are selections from his instructions, which are written in prose of the most exceptional grace and beauty, adding a matchless artistic quality to the scientific precision found in corresponding works of Yuanwu, Foyan, and Dahui.

In his teachings on mental freedom, Hongzhi affirmed that the mind is originally unattached to objects. To actualize this as a practical affair, however, he taught what he calls the "silent exercise of inner gazing." He reiterates the Zen dictum that there is no way to explain reality, that it must be experienced on one's own; to do this, he said, "Just wash away the dust and dirt of subjective thoughts immediately." Success in this allows the practitioner to progress to an effortless type of Zen exercise in which there is spontaneous awareness and panoramic consciousness.

Enlightened life, Hongzhi writes, is natural and spontaneous, yet orderly and not arbitrary. He presents exercises for eliminating arbitrariness and perfecting attunement of the human mind, keeping this true inward spirituality intact even while participating in the ordinary world. Dahui maintained that when quiet sitting does not result in serenity in the midst of turbulence, that means it is not really effective even in quietude; similarly, Hongzhi criticized some students for sitting in meditation too long and losing the capacity for effective integration.

The selections from Hongzhi's work translated in this volume are followed by excerpts from the instructions of Ying-an, another distinguished teacher from the East Mountain School. Ying-an became a disciple of the great Yuanwu after having had an initial enlightenment under the tutelage of another Zen master. Later, on Yuanwu's own recommendation, Ying-an became a student of Huqiu, one of Yuanwu's successors, known as the "Sleeping Tiger" of Yuanwu's circle. Huqiu eventually recognized Ying-an as a Zen master and gave him permission to teach.

In his presentation of Zen, Ying-an emphasized immunity to the ordinary economic, social, and mental influences that ordinarily coerce humanity. Zen freedom, he said, cannot be pinned down and cannot be second-guessed. Real perception is the essence of Zen, he maintained; genuine Zen students have no resorts, no fixed creed or religion.

Ying-an cites several types of degenerate Zen, including those deriving from attachment to temporary insights and isolated elaborations of limited views. He also describes multiple personalities of both quietism and nihilism, which sometimes masquerade as Zen. One type of false Zen is characterized by Ying-an as promoted by people whose minds have been poisoned by false teachers into thinking that they are themselves Zen masters. Another type of false Zen is promoted by camp followers who pick up Zen lingo and try to become known for their Zennism. To be cured of these forms of madness, people may need to give up deliberate involvement in spiritual studies.

A familiar Taoist proverb says, "The journey of a thousand miles begins with the first step." According to Ying-an, the first step must be the right step, in the right direction, if it is to lead to arrival at the destination. This is why ancient Zen masters left behind so many directions, or at least indications as to how and where seekers might find direction.

In his instructions, Ying-an also notes that eagerness to learn is often a prime barrier to real Zen perception. Not the least of the drawbacks of such eagerness is that it may foster the impulsive tendency to take the "first step of a thousand mile journey" at random. Don't approach Zen with preconceptions, Ying-an teaches, yet don't think there is no Zen understanding. It takes practice, he says, but the purpose of the practice is to arrive at naturalness and spontaneity.

One of the most general observations made by Zen masters is that activities that once had a specific purpose tend to be diverted to other purposes or transformed into ends in themselves. Virtually all of the methods of Zen that can be defined have been thus diverted or transformed at various times, as have most ordinary educational methods. This is one reason for periodic changes in tactics.

"Zen cannot be attained by lectures, discussions, or debates," says Ying-an, referring no doubt to the highly ritualized remnants of interactional education popularized in baroque Zen schools. On the other hand, he continues, if people can do as the ancient Zen masters themselves did, "at some point you will suddenly turn the light of your mind around and see through illusions to the real self."

Overly intellectualized versions of quasi Zen evidently abounded in Song-dynasty China, undoubtedly contributing to the ossification of such formats as those Ying-an renounced. Of the desire for intellectual knowledge, Ying-an says, "Your chills and fever will be increased by the wind of intellectual knowledge, your nose will always be stuffed up and your head will always be foggy."

Many of the stumbling blocks and blind alleys that Ying-an notes are related in some way either to excessively intellectual or anti-intellectual approaches to Zen. Intellectualism is found among many academic, literary, artistic, and priestly attitudes toward Zen; but then again so is anti-intellectualism, or the idea that because Zen denies the supremacy of intellect it must be anti-intellectual.

Ying-an also reemphasizes the point that people interested in Zen should not approach it with the idea of achieving greatness, or with eagerness for success, or with desire for recognition. According to Zen teaching, all of this is the work of vanity, not real aspiration for enlightenment. It is therefore counterproductive and blocks the way of Zen.

Because Zen enlightenment is ultimately beyond words, teachers have been known to use other means of communicating impressions. Among the more dramatic of their techniques were various shock tactics. Surprising blows and shouts, for example, are known to have been employed by some ancient Zen masters to produce specific effects in the minds of seekers. These devices are also known to have been widely mimed. Used imitatively and at random, they lost their original intended effects. Thus they were transformed into forms of pretense and mystification. There are many references to this phenomenon in Zen literature.

Ying-an says that blows and shouts—which in the popular mind came to be associated with Zen mysticism—do not really represent Zen. Instead of being concerned with doctrines, literary expressions, or pantomime, Ying-an recommends what he calls "a certain state in which no time whatsoever is wasted, twenty-four hours a day," a state to be "maintained until you reach the point where there is nowhere to grasp and nowhere to anchor."

Then, he says, "You should let go and make yourself empty and quiet, clear and calm, to the point where former intellectual interpretations, rationalizations, misknowledge and misperception, cannot get into your mind or act on it at all." Ying-an also stresses the need for a strong will to accomplish this; even though seeing the Zen mind is easy, he said, strength is needed to use it.

Following the sayings of Ying-an in this collection are extracts from the talks of one of his Zen successors, master Mi-an. According to Mi-an, Zen is a matter of being "totally alive and free," for only thus is it possible to be in the world without being affected by it. This possibility is inherent in everyone, he says, but many people who try to attain it through Zen are misled by false teachers. When Zen study is also motivated by a desire for recognition, he warns, this makes people so much the more susceptible to such deception.

Mi-an cites half a dozen typical problems that inhibit Zen enlightenment in spite of intensive study. He adds that these are problems encountered not only by beginners, but even by people with basic Zen experience. Mi-an emphasizes, however, that when Zen is realized, "Buddhist truths and things of the world have become one— where is there any external thing to constitute an impediment?"

Mi-an's sayings are followed by Zen instructions of Xiatang, another of Yuanwu's noted disciples. Xiatang gives a detailed explanation of nondiscursive knowledge, considered basic to Zen. He points out that the awareness in this knowledge is inherently nondiscursive; it is not reached by suppression of reason, but by a level of attention beyond that of ordinary sense. Xiatang also hints that the source of awareness is in fact the "spiritual immortality" sought by the higher ranks of Taoists.

Xiatang makes it clear, however, that attaining experience of this nondiscursive knowledge is not the same thing as utilizing it. "Glimpsing" followed by obsession spells trouble, he says, using the classic metaphor of "gold dust in the eyes" to describe the problem of spiritual attachment. As usual, Xiatang also quotes ancient masters on ways out of this impasse.

Xiatang stresses the primary importance of breaking the hold of compulsive or coercive habituation and conditioning mechanisms. He follows this up with emphasis on the need to be aware of the consequences of actions. The realm beyond the tyranny of external influences is sometimes called emptiness, or nothingness, in the sense that reality is seen without a mind full of preconceptions.

Many of the Song dynasty Zen masters urgently addressed the attitudinal and behavioral problems associated with imperfect realization of emptiness. A later master explained that the Zen stage of "no good or evil" does not mean that evil is good, and does not mean that one can do ill and not suffer the consequences. It means, he said, that one is not touched by either good or evil. Only then, according to classical Zen teaching, is one capable of distinguishing real good and evil from supposed good and evil, without subjective biases implanted by conditioning.

This volume concludes with excerpts from the sayings of Yuansou, one of the most illustrious Zen masters of the fourteenth century. At this time China was ruled by Mongol usurpers, who generally favored the Tibetan schools of Buddhism over the Chinese schools. Kubilai Khan (grandson of the notorious Jenghiz Khan), who extended the Mongol conquest to include the whole of continental China, was for a time interested in Zen Buddhism, but few Mongolians seem to have gone into Zen studies. One of the rare Mongolian Zen masters, however, was a student of Yuansou.

Yuansou was a fourth generation heir of the Zen lineage of the great Dahui, but he also worked with one of the last masters of Hongzhi's line as well. Yuansou is said to have given many evidences of paranormal powers, and he attracted thousands of seekers during his many years as a public teacher. Although much of the record of his teaching is said to have been lost during the civil disturbances of the latter fourteenth century as the Mongolian Yuan dynasty crumbled, nevertheless a considerable amount of material has survived, including a number of instructional letters, from which the present selections are translated.

Yuansou presents a fairly detailed description of the essence of Zen meditation, showing how different terms used through the ages refer to the same thing. He emphasizes the expedient nature of the Buddhist teachings, noting something of their wide variety. He also mentions a number of very general and very common approaches to Zen realization, and states that the aim is not actually confined to, or within, any particular approach.

Yuansou confirms the elusive omnipresence of Zen experience, which is made elusive only by attempts to pin it down. Yuansou says that when you try to pin Zen down, it pins you down; as you allow yourself to be "misled by blind teachers into reifying Buddha, Dharma, Zen, Tao, mysteries, marvels, functions, and states, one way and another this glues your tongue down, nails your eyes shut, and constricts your heart."

Explaining the reasons for use of expedient methods, Yuansou says that the "various teachings and techniques of Buddhas and Zen masters are only set forth so that you will individually step back into yourself, understand your own original mind and see your original nature, so that you reach a state of great rest, peace, and happiness."

Adding that accumulated bad habits hinder people along the way, Yuansou warns that just as this is true in ordinary life it is even more so when trying to reach sophisticated Zen perceptions, which cannot be consciously arranged even with good intentions. What is more, he says, bad habits may well lay beneath a veneer of good intentions. This is the pattern of pretended religionists and spiritual hobbyists characterized by Yuansou in these terms: "You pick up your baggage and go to other people's houses looking for Zen, looking for Tao, looking for mysteries, looking for marvels, looking for buddhas, looking for Zen masters, looking for teachers. You think this is searching for the ultimate and make it into your religion, but this is like running blindly to the east to get something in the west. The more you run the further away you are, and the more you hurry the later you become."

Yuansou also speaks of the straightforwardness of Zen mind, unburdened by confusing and deluding thoughts and ideas. He says it is impersonal and does not belong to any culture or system or idea. Subjectivity in discrimination, he warns, grasping and rejecting, makes people lose their independence and fall under the mesmeric influence of "things." Thus from first to last his total emphasis, like that of all the classical Zen masters, is on liberation—the freedom to see, the freedom to be, the freedom to live deliberately.

(Continued on next page)

The Shambhala Dictionary of Buddhism and Zen.

The Spiritual Teaching of Ramana Maharshi, by Ramana Maharshi. Foreword by C. G. Jung.

Tao Teh Ching, by Lao Tzu. Translated by John C. H. Wu.

The Tibetan Book of the Dead: The Great Liberation through Hearing in the Bardo. Translated with commentary of Francesca Fremantle & Chögyam Trungpa.

Vitality, Energy, Spirit: A Taoist Sourcebook. Translated & edited by Thomas Cleary.

Wen-tzu: Understanding the Mysteries, by Lao-tzu. Translated by Thomas Cleary.

Worldly Wisdom: Confucian Teachings of the Ming Dynasty. Translated & edited by J. C. Cleary.

Zen Essence: The Science of Freedom. Translated & edited by Thomas Cleary.

The Zen Teachings of Master Lin-chi. Translated by Burton Watson.

20295559R00079

Made in the USA
Lexington, KY
29 January 2013